17 Proven Currency Trading Strategies

Founded in 1807, John Wiley & Sons is the oldest independent publishing company in the United States. With offices in North America, Europe, Australia, and Asia, Wiley is globally committed to developing and marketing print and electronic products and services for our customers' professional and personal knowledge and understanding.

The Wiley Trading series features books by traders who have survived the market's ever-changing temperament and have prospered—some by reinventing systems, others by getting back to basics. Whether you are a novice trader, professional, or somewhere in between, these books will provide the advice and strategies needed to prosper today and well into the future.

For a list of available titles, visit our website at www.WileyFinance.com.

17 Proven Currency Trading Strategies

How to Profit in the Forex Market

MARIO SINGH

WILEY

John Wiley & Sons Singapore Pte. Ltd.

Other Wiley Editorial Offices
John Wiley & Sons, 111 River Street, Hoboken, NJ 07030, USA
John Wiley & Sons, The Atrium, Southern Gate, Chichester, West Sussex, P019 8SQ, United Kingdom
John Wiley & Sons (Canada) Ltd., 5353 Dundas Street West, Suite 400, Toronto, Ontario, M9B 6HB, Canada
John Wiley & Sons Australia Ltd., 42 McDougall Street, Milton, Queensland 4064, Australia
Wiley-VCH, Boschstrasse 12, D-69469 Weinheim, Germany

ISBN 978–1–118–38551–7 (Cloth)
ISBN 978–1–118–38553–1 (ePDF)
ISBN 978–1–118–38554–8 (Mobi)
ISBN 978–1–118–38552–4 (ePub)

Typeset in 10/12 pt, ITC Century by MPS Limited, Chennai, India.

10 9 8 7 6 5 4 3 2 1

To my three angels:
Shalyn, my beautiful soul mate
Chantelle, my vivacious daughter
Elliot, my bubbly son

Thank you for showing me every day that while
the forex market holds the key to abundant wealth, my true treasure
is found in the three of you.

I love you with all my heart.

Contents

Preface

You can't afford to ignore forex anymore.

This is an urgent message I carry everywhere I go. It really doesn't matter who we are or what stage in life we're at. You could be in school and you can't seem to figure out the rules of global finance. You could be holding down a job but you desire to make a decent second income in your spare time.

You could already be involved in the financial markets as a retail trader or investor, but with low yields and depressed growth all around the world, you are searching for an asset class that offers unparalleled returns. You might even be a fund manager who holds an international portfolio in different asset classes, such as equities, bonds, and commodities.

However, with central banks lowering rates and injecting record amounts of liquidity into the financial system, you realize the importance of protecting your entire portfolio against currency risks.

Finally, you might be someone running a multinational company. You could be based in one country, but your offices span across many countries all around the world. Expenses for salaries, infrastructure, machinery, and supplies are paid out in different currencies every single month. As the business gets larger, you can't turn a blind eye to the currency fluctuations, which have a significant impact to the company's bottom line every month.

If you find yourself in any one of these categories, this book is for you. The sooner we all understand the forex "game," the better it is going to be for us. Forex is a game for three reasons. First, playing it must be fun. Second, we play it with an intention to win. Finally, it has rules. If you break the rules, the rules will break you.

HOW IT ALL BEGAN

I had a painful start to forex trading because I broke a cardinal rule. Allow me to share my story with you. I'll be the first to admit that I'm not a smart guy. I don't have a finance degree or an economics degree.

I studied chemical engineering in school but graduated with third-class honors, dashing my mother's hopes of my becoming a top chief executive for a Fortune 500 company. After graduation, I proceeded to apply for a job at petroleum giant Shell, but I haven't heard from them yet.

Sometimes I console myself by thinking that my resume lost its way in the mail. I didn't have much materially then, but what I had was the burning desire to achieve success in life. It was this desire to succeed that led me to my first experience with forex trading.

Six years ago, I was with a friend in a local coffee shop when he suddenly flipped open his laptop to reveal a screen full of charts. Through the charts and jumping numbers on the screen, I asked him, "What's this?"

He coolly replied, "Forex trading."

Thinking it was some hobby he recently picked up, I asked again, "Real cash?"

"Yes." He nodded smugly. "Real cash."

That began to draw me in, slowly but surely. Looking back, it wasn't the fact that forex was the biggest financial market in the world that drew me in. What drew me in was the fact that all you needed was an Internet connection and a laptop to make money from this market anywhere in the world.

Fascinated, I started to ask my trader friend some questions. When he shared with me the story of how George Soros broke the Bank of England on September 16, 1992, and made $1 billion in a day, I was hooked.

I'm the kind of guy who only needs one live example of someone who has done something to convince me that I can do it too. Excited about this new discovery called forex trading, I went off and started to do my own reading on free websites.

Soon I started my first account with USD3,000.

MY FIRST TRADE

My first trade was on the GBP/USD. It was on an uptrend, and the price had reached a new high. This is it, I thought, rubbing my hands gleefully. I'm going to be a millionaire by next Friday. Seeing that the price had reached a new high, I was convinced that gravity would pull it right down.

I clicked "sell." That poignant moment was the start of my painful lesson. After I clicked "sell," the price continued to creep up. That's not supposed to happen, I thought.

As prices continued climbing, I decided to hit the sell button again, only this time with double the lot size (and double the intensity) as my first trade. I reasoned that if I clicked twice the number of lots, all that needed to happen was for prices to fall a little before I could see some nice profits.

After the second "sell" click, I couldn't believe my eyes. The price went up further. My hands started to get sweaty. My head started to shine from the beads of sweat that started to trickle down from my bald head. Murphy's Law was in full motion. In desperation, I actually grabbed the laptop and turned it upside down to paint me a picture of falling prices. My ego was badly hurt.

"It's got to come down," I muttered to myself. At that point, I clicked "sell" for a third time, with double the lot size of the second trade.

The numbers on my laptop screen at the time weren't very far from the numbers my friend had shown me. The only difference was that mine had a stubborn negative sign preceding them that just wouldn't go away. A couple of days after my third dreaded click, the broker closed off all my positions. I was hit with the dreaded margin call.

In a grand total of just six days, I had lost my entire account.

Whenever I share my story in my forex seminars, I replicate the scenario and draw an uptrend on the whiteboard.

"Would you click 'buy' or 'sell' over here?" I always ask, as I circle the highest point reached by the price. At every single seminar, most people choose to sell, confident that high prices will fall.

It's almost a consolation to know that we human beings are wired in much the same way. Needless to say, after I blew up my account, I was devastated.

THERE ARE NO SUCCESSFUL BUSINESSES

Losing USD3,000 of my hard-earned money in a week was heart-wrenching.

Self-defeating thoughts appeared in my mind incessantly.

"Forex is risky."

"Forex is gambling."

"Forex is not for me."

I was tempted to wash my hands from the forex market and walk away.

However, it was at this low point of my life that the words of a rich and successful Chinese businessman who was my mentor came to mind.

世界上没有成功的事业，只有成功的人。

"There are no successful businesses in this world, only successful people."

At this point, I stopped the pity party and asked myself two questions: *Do I know people who are making money in the forex market?* And: *Do I want to be in that group?*

I picked myself up again after I answered yes to both questions. I started to work on myself. You see, it's very easy for you and me to get sucked into recognizing that 80% of people lose money in the forex market.

However, why can't we decide to be in the group that makes money? Isn't it just a simple switch in our thinking? If 20% of the people are making money, let's decide first to have our names in that special group. That self-talk was the turning point in my forex trading journey. I made up my mind to master forex trading.

Picking myself up from the setback, I began to equip myself with the right trading skills. I started devouring books by successful traders. Emulating their beliefs, knowledge, and habits, I worked hard on honing my trading skills every single day. My quest for mastery also led me to seek out two of the biggest names in the forex industry as my mentors: Kathy Lien and Ed Ponsi.

I reasoned that a mentor could help me to drastically cut short my learning curve. And cut short my learning curve they did.

Knowing what I know now, I recognize that the cardinal rule that I broke in my first live trading experience was to trade against the trend.

Within three years and several buckets of blood, sweat and tears later, I became an expert in trading the forex market. Less than a year later, I was invited to appear on CNBC to give my opinions on global finance.

WISH THAT YOU WERE BETTER

Given my bubbly character, many people think that it's easy being on camera, speaking live to a camera that holds the attention of over 300 million viewers. The truth for me is that it's not.

"Mario, what do you think the CPI is going to be for Singapore?"

"Mario, what's your view on the U.S. dollar this week?"

"Mario, do you think China will report a good number for trade surplus this month?"

The TV anchor and the reporters on site fire questions from every angle, and you need to have the answers at your fingertips. They expect you to know, or you have no business being on the biggest stage in international finance.

How ridiculous it would be if I were to fake an answer like "I think inflation in Singapore is going to hit 65% next year." I would be laughed off the chair.

So I had to study. In fact, to be in that three-minute hot seat, I had to study for three hours. That's right: three full hours of study for three minutes on CNBC.

Thankfully, I did well. In fact, I did so well that I was called back, again and again. CNBC has three major shows that cover the financial markets. The early morning segment is called *Squawk Box*, in the early afternoon it's called *Capital Connection,* and the evening's slot is called *Worldwide Exchange.*

Eventually I was invited to appear on all three major shows. In fact, I was then asked to be a guest host on *Worldwide Exchange.* As guest host, I sat with the news anchor and instead of being there for three minutes, I would be there for a full hour.

My job was to have a conversation with some of the most brilliant financial minds on the planet who would come in and take their place on the hot seat. As I warmed up to the new role as a guest host, I had an important revelation. The job was getting easier. In fact, I didn't have to study when I was guest host.

Do you know why? Because this time, it was my turn to ask the all-important question, "So, Jack, what's your view on the U.S. dollar this week?"

This was my revelation: As you get better, it gets easier.

So, my friend, don't wish that it were easier, wish that you were better.

Kaizen is the Japanese word for improvement. When we embrace *kaizen* in any endeavor, mastery is bound to be the result.

My *kaizen* approach to forex trading has enabled me to be a consistently profitable trader. Today, I am living the dream of traveling and spreading the message of profitable forex trading everywhere I go. I've even had the privilege to coach forex traders in some of the largest banks in the world. Forex trading has given me this new life, and I know that it can do the same for you.

AUDIENCE

Today the Forex Market is considered the largest financial market in the world. With that famous tagline, thousands of books have sprung up giving people insights into this amazing market. I did not write this book with the intention of adding to the vast list of global resources already available on the topic of forex.

My inspiration for this book is drawn from three specific groups of people:

1. All forex traders around the world. It is my humble wish that this book will become the platinum standard in forex education. The rich content here will suit you regardless of which stage you are in your trading career: beginner, intermediate, or advanced. Pay particular attention to Chapter 5, which puts you through a fun and interesting quiz. At the

end of the quiz, you will discover which one of the five categories of traders you belong to. If you stick to the strategies pertinent to your profile, you will be pleasantly surprised by the results.

2. Finance and business professionals who are not currently involved in the forex market. You may be involved in equities, fixed-income instruments, or commodities. An understanding of global finance and forex movements will greatly help you in your decision making. Remember, capital flows into a country first, before it flows into any specific asset class. An understanding of the forex market puts you in prime position to anticipate these flows. Chapter 3 is dedicated to business corporations that must understand the importance of hedging. Hedging helps corporations gain certainty of price, even when payments are made or received in different currencies. Hedging thus helps corporations to mitigate the foreign exchange risk exposure.

3. Ordinary folks outside of the finance industry who are looking to create a powerful second income. With a potent combination of unprecedented liquidity and sovereign debt levels in the world today, there truly has never been a better time to get involved in forex. I ask you humbly to consider this opportunity.

OVERVIEW OF THE CONTENTS

The book is broken into two parts:

Part One: Forex Is a Game

Part One of this book is divided into five chapters, and it centers on the core description of forex as a game. We discover insights on the rules of the game, the major players, and how money is made.

Chapter 1 introduces the forex market. It begins by describing the total daily turnover and the seven major currency pairs. It then explains how to read a forex quote and how prices move. The chapter ends with a framework of how margin and leverage are employed in a forex trade.

Chapter 2 focuses on how money is made in a forex trade. We learn about long and short and the three points in every trade. We then move to the four big reasons that cause currencies to move and get a grasp of the fraction theory. Chapter 2 ends with an understanding of market structure.

Chapters 3 and 4 cover the six major players in the forex market and the numerous advantages associated with trading the market. Some of the major players include central banks, commercial banks, multinational companies, and retail traders. We also get a glimpse of three of the biggest blow-ups in proprietary trading in banking history.

Chapter 5 is devoted to discovering your unique profile in trading. It includes a profiling test to help you find out how your personality can help or hurt your trading style. There are essentially five types of traders: scalper, day trader, swing trader, position trader, and mechanical trader. By the end of this chapter, you will know which group you belong to.

Part Two: Strategies to Win the Game

Part Two is also divided into five chapters. Each chapter covers strategies for the five profiles of scalper, day trader, swing trader, position trader, and mechanical trader.

Chapter 6 covers two strategies for scalpers, called the rapid fire and the piranha. These strategies are used on the shortest time frames, namely the minute chart and the 5-minute chart.

Chapter 7 covers four strategies for day traders. The first two strategies are focused on breakouts while the next two are centered purely on trading the news. A unique way of trading the news, called the Rule of 20, is also discussed here. All four strategies are employed using the 15-minute and 30-minute time frame.

Chapter 8 covers five strategies for swing traders. As swing traders typically exit their positions within two to five days, the time frames used for the strategies are longer than the day traders. Hence, all five of the swing trading strategies are used on the 1-hour and the 4-hour time frame.

Chapter 9 covers three strategies for position traders. The first one, swap and fly, takes advantage of the interest rate differentials between the currencies and aims to earn maximum returns by holding on to positions for an extended period of time. The next two strategies are used specifically for the two most popular commodities in the world: oil and gold.

The final chapter covers three strategies for mechanical traders. Traders in this category are oblivious to the passing of time. This is why all strategies discussed here employ three different time frames from the other categories: the 5-minute chart, the 15-minute chart, and the daily chart.

Acknowledgments

My heartfelt thanks to the following people, without whom this book would not have been possible:

My coaches at FX1 Academy, Muhammad Fadzali, Tim Sim Yong Siang, and Ko Heng Whye. Thank you for burning countless hours with me to ensure the content and charts were in order. I will remember the mountain of McDonald's burgers we had together during the process.

Terry Thompson, president of FXPRIMUS. Thank you for graciously allowing me to use all the charts from the FXPRIMUS MT4 Platform.

Jeff Zweig, director of Digital Strategy at FXPRIMUS. Thank you for your brilliant ideas in ensuring that this book reached the four corners of the earth.

The awesome team at Wiley: Nick Melchior, Cynthia Mak, Gemma Rosey, and Sharifah Sharomsah. Thank you for your pursuit of excellence and for sharing my excitement in getting this book out to the world.

My forex mentors, Ed Ponsi and Kathy Lien. Thank you for shaping my thoughts early on in my trading career. Yes, news does matter.

All budding and existing traders worldwide. Thank you for keeping the forex flame burning bright. You are the driving force that propels me to share my knowledge and experience of forex trading all over the world.

To Almighty God, thank you for teaching me to dream big and to understand that I am more than a conqueror.

PART ONE

Forex Is a Game

C hapter 1 introduces the forex market. It begins by describing the total daily turnover and the seven major currency pairs. It then explains how to read a forex quote and how prices move. The chapter ends with a framework of how margin and leverage are employed in a forex trade.

Chapter 2 focuses on how money is made in a forex trade. We learn about long and short and the three points in every trade. We then move to the four big reasons that cause currencies to move and get a grasp of the fraction theory. Chapter 2 ends with an understanding of market structure.

Chapters 3 and 4 cover the six major players in the forex market and the numerous advantages associated with trading the market. Some of the major players include central banks, commercial banks, multinational companies, and retail traders. We also get a glimpse of three of the biggest blow-ups in proprietary trading in banking history.

Chapter 5 is devoted to discovering your unique profile in trading. It includes a profiling test to help you find out how your personality can help or hurt your trading style. There are essentially five types of traders: scalper, day trader, swing trader, position trader, and mechanical trader. By the end of this chapter, you will know which group you belong to.

CHAPTER 1

How to Play the Game

This chapter presents some of the essentials that you must know when you start trading the forex market. In it we describe the seven major currency pairs that are most commonly traded worldwide and explain how prices move. We also discuss the yen factor, which quotes forex prices in two decimal places as opposed to the normal four. The final part of the chapter defines the value of a pip and explains how margin and leverage affect trades.

THE FOREX GAME

The forex game has changed much over the years. Today, it is undisputedly the largest financial market in the world, with a daily trading volume in excess of USD4 trillion. The authoritative source on global forex market activity is the Triennial Central Bank Survey of Foreign Exchange and Derivatives Market Activity, published by the Bank for International Settlements (BIS).

Available official figures for daily forex turnover are taken from the last survey done in April 2010. Fifty-three central banks and monetary authorities participated in the survey, collecting information from 1,309 market participants.

An excerpt from the BIS report reads:

The 2010 triennial survey shows another significant increase in global foreign exchange market activity since the last survey in 2007, following the unprecedented rise in activity between 2004 and 2007. Global foreign exchange market turnover was 20% higher in April 2010 than in April 2007. This increase brought average daily turnover to USD4.0 trillion (from USD3.3 trillion) at current exchange rates.

http://www.bis.org/publ/rpfx10.htm

At the heart of the report, an interesting fact stood out. Apparently, 48% of the growth was in spot transactions, which represented 37% of the total turnover of forex transactions worldwide. Spot transactions are mostly traded by retail traders—that's everyday people like you and me. This group is rapidly expanding and is expected to contribute an even larger portion of total forex turnover by the time the next survey is out.

This Triennial Survey is done once every three years, and the next one is due in April 2013. Publication of preliminary results will follow four months later. The official figure for daily forex turnover is expected to be well over USD4 trillion at that time. Figure 1.1 shows the breakdown of the daily turnover by instrument.

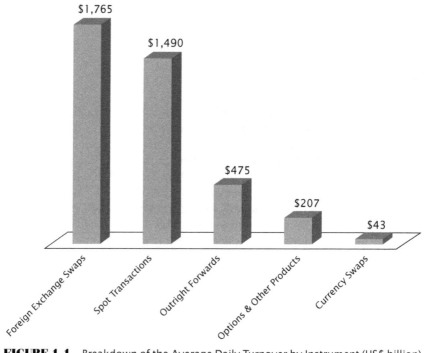

FIGURE 1.1   Breakdown of the Average Daily Turnover by Instrument (US$ billion)
Source: Bank for International Settlements, September 2010

The USD4 trillion daily turnover on the forex market is truly staggering. According to the April 2010 BIS Triennial Survey, this figure is:

- More than 23 times the average daily turnover of global equity markets
- More than 40 times the annual turnover of world gross domestic product

In fact, in the latest *BIS Quarterly Review*, dated March 2012, Morten Bech, senior economist in the Monetary and Economics Department of BIS, estimated that "global FX activity was around $4.7 trillion a day on average in October 2011, compared with $4.0 trillion reported by the latest triennial central bank survey of foreign exchange activity conducted in April 2010."

Imagine that: USD4.7 trillion in a day on average in October 2011!

It certainly won't be surprising to see the figure top the USD5 trillion mark when the official figures are released from the April 2013 survey. The good news for the retail trader is this: As a result of increasing demand, transaction costs such as spreads have decreased, technology offerings have improved, and value-added services on forex brokerage firms have exploded.

There truly never has been a better time to start trading on the forex market. This exciting message is further reinforced by the record numbers of everyday folks—people like you and me—who continue to jump onboard the forex bandwagon at an accelerated pace.

FOREX AND THE SEVEN MAJORS

Foreign exchange, or forex for short, is a market where one currency is exchanged for another. This is the reason why forex is quoted in currency pairs. Each world currency is given a three-letter code as set out by the International Standards Organization (ISO) and governed by the ISO 4217.

The eight most commonly traded currencies are:

1. USD (U.S. dollar)
2. EUR (euros)
3. GBP (Great Britain pound)
4. AUD (Australian dollar)
5. JPY (Japanese yen)
6. CHF (Swiss franc)
7. CAD (Canadian dollar)
8. NZD (New Zealand dollar)

The eight most commonly traded currencies form the seven major currency pairs. These seven majors dominate the forex market in terms of traded volume. Since January 2012, it is estimated that the seven majors account for over 85% of the daily traded volume in the forex market.

These seven major currency pairs are:

1. EUR/USD: euro versus U.S. dollar
2. USD/JPY: U.S. dollar versus Japanese yen
3. GBP/USD: Great Britain pound versus U.S. dollar
4. AUD/USD: Australian dollar versus U.S. dollar
5. USD/CHF: U.S. dollar versus Swiss franc
6. USD/CAD: U.S. dollar versus Canadian dollar
7. NZD/USD: New Zealand dollar versus U.S. dollar

Figure 1.2 shows how much volume is contributed by the seven majors. It also shows that the EUR/USD currency pair contributes the highest percentage of daily traded volume, with 28%.

For all of the listed seven majors, the U.S. dollar features in either the left-hand side or the right-hand side of the currency pair. This is why the U.S. dollar is the most liquid currency in the forex world.

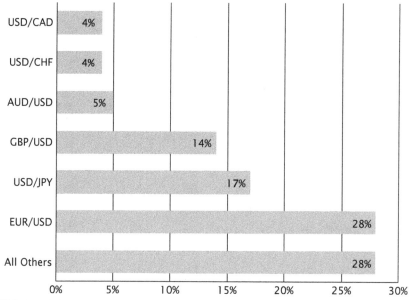

FIGURE 1.2   Daily Traded Volume Contributed by the Major Currency Pairs

Reading a Forex Quote

Forex prices are quoted in currency pairs and almost always to four decimal places. For example, if a forex quote is given as EUR/USD = 1.3255, the currency on the left is termed the "base currency" while the currency on the right is termed the "counter currency." The base currency always has a value of 1. In the example, the euro is the base currency while the U.S. dollar is the counter currency. This is how we would read the forex quote: *1 euro is equivalent to 1.3255 U.S. dollars at that point of time.*

This forex quote tells us two things. First, if traders are eager to purchase one unit of the base currency, they would have to pay 1.3255 U.S. dollars to buy 1 euro. If, however, traders are eager to sell one unit of the base currency, they would receive 1.3255 U.S. dollars for selling 1 euro. It is also important to note that the exchange rate always fluctuates with changing market conditions. At any time, the euro can weaken or strengthen against the U.S. dollar.

If the EUR/USD quote moves up from 1.3255 to 1.3287, the euro is strengthening against the U.S. dollar. However, if the EUR/USD quote moves down from 1.3255 to 1.3138, the euro is weakening against the U.S. dollar.

The Yen Factor

Not all forex quotes are created equal, especially when it comes to the Japanese yen. Whenever the Japanese yen is in the counter currency, the forex quote is given in two decimal places instead of four. Let's take a look at an example.

USD/JPY = 80.55

The quote tells us that 1 U.S. dollar is equivalent to 80.55 Japanese yen at that point of time.

If the USD/JPY quote moves up from 80.55 to 80.87, the U.S. dollar is strengthening against the Japanese yen. If the USD/JPY quote moves down from 80.55 to 79.78, the U.S. dollar is weakening against the Japanese yen.

Pip

Pip stands for "price interest point." It is the unit of measurement to express the change in value between two currencies.

Let's say that the current AUD/USD price is 1.0235. If the price rises to 1.0236 or falls to 1.0234, this is a movement of 0.0001, or 1 pip. If the current price of USD/JPY is 81.33, and if the price rises to 81.34 or falls to 81.32, this is a movement of 0.01, or 1 pip.

One pip is thus the smallest change in value for any given forex quote, whether it's quoted to two or four decimal places. Here are more examples:

- When the EUR/USD quote moves up from 1.3255 to 1.3287, it is a movement of 32 pips.

  When the EUR/USD quote moves down from 1.3255 to 1.3138, it is a movement of 117 pips.

- When the USD/CHF quote moves up from 0.9148 to 0.9263, it is a movement of 115 pips.

  When the USD/CHF quote moves down from 0.9148 to 0.9126, it is a movement of 22 pips.

- When the USD/JPY quote moves up from 80.55 to 80.87, it is a movement of 32 pips.

  When the USD/JPY quote moves down from 80.55 to 79.78, it is a movement of 77 pips.

Pipette   Many brokers today extend forex quotes beyond the standard four and two decimal places, to five and three decimal places respectively. As an example, a broker could quote USD/CAD as 1.00583. If the USD/CAD quote rises to either 1.00584 or falls to 1.00582, the movement is termed 1 pipette.

Similarly, if USD/JPY is quoted as 81.338 and if the currency pair rises to either 81.339 or falls to 81.337, the movement is termed 1 pipette as well.

How Do We Calculate the Value Of One Pip?   Different currencies have different values. Hence, the value of a pip is different for each currency.

The first thing to take note of when calculating pip value is that for most forex quotes, particularly the seven majors, the U.S. dollar is either the base currency or the counter currency.

In the USD/CHF quote, the U.S. dollar is the base currency. In the AUD/USD quote, the U.S. dollar is the counter currency.

Let's calculate the pip value for each example, starting with the U.S. dollar as the base currency (see Examples 1.1 and 1.2).

EXAMPLE 1.1: VALUE OF 1 PIP

Let's take the current price of USD/CHF as 0.9235. The smallest movement for a pip is thus 0.0001.
The formula for calculating pip value is:

Pip value = Smallest decimal move/Current exchange rate
= 0.0001/0.9235
= **0.000108**

The value of 1 pip when the USD/CHF is at 0.9235 is USD 0.000108.
To determine the pip value for Japanese yen pairs, let's take a look at the next example.
If the current price of USD/JPY is 81.55, the smallest movement for a pip is 0.01.
The formula for calculating pip value is:

Pip value = Smallest decimal move/Current exchange rate
= 0.01/81.55
= **0.000123**

The value of 1 pip when the USD/JPY is at 81.55 is USD 0.000123.

EXAMPLE 1.2: VALUE OF 1 PIP

Let's take a look at how pip value is determined when the U.S. dollar is the counter currency.
If the AUD/USD is now 1.0237, then:

Pip value = Smallest decimal move/Current exchange rate
= 0.0001/1.0237
= **0.00009768**

The value of 1 pip when the AUD/USD is at 1.0237 is AUD 0.00009768. Take note that in this case, the value of 1 pip is quoted in Australian dollars (AUD).
To find out the value of 1 pip in U.S. dollars, we simply take the current pip value and multiply it by the current exchange rate:

Pip value (in USD) = Pip value (in base currency) × Current exchange rate
= 0.00009768 × 1.0237
= 0.0001

Thus, the value of 1 pip when the AUD/USD is at 1.0237 is USD 0.0001.
Although the process may look complicated, the good news is that every single broker you trade with will calculate this value automatically for you.

Lot Size Most forex brokers today provide up to four categories of lot sizes for the trader. These are:

1. Standard lot
2. Mini lot
3. Micro lot
4. Nano lot

A standard lot is defined as 100,000 units of the base currency. For an example, when you buy 1 standard lot of EUR/USD, you are purchasing 100,000 euros with U.S. dollars.

A mini lot is defined as 10,000 units of the base currency. For an example, when you buy 1 mini lot of GBP/USD, you are purchasing 10,000 pounds with U.S. dollars.

A micro lot is defined as 1,000 units of the base currency. For an example, when you buy 1 micro lot of USD/CHF, you are purchasing 1,000 U.S. dollars with Swiss francs.

A nano lot is defined as 100 units of the base currency. For an example, when you buy 1 nano lot of USD/CAD, you are purchasing 100 U.S. dollars with Canadian dollars.

The lot size decreases by a factor of 10 from standard, to mini, to micro, and finally to nano, as shown in Table 1.1.

Standard Lot

If you trade standard lots, then, using the same values as Example 1.1:

$$USD/CHF = 0.9235$$

$$Pip\ value = USD\ 0.000108$$

$$Pip\ value\ for\ standard\ lot = USD\ 0.000108 \times 100,000$$

$$= USD\ 10.80$$

TABLE 1.1 Four Categories of Lot Sizes

Lot Size Category	Number of Units
Standard	100,000
Mini	10,000
Micro	1,000
Nano	100

Looking at the USD/JPY example with quotes to two decimal places:

$$USD/JPY = 81.55$$
$$\text{Pip value} = USD\ 0.000123$$
$$\text{Pip value for standard lot} = USD\ 0.000123 \times 100{,}000$$
$$= USD\ 12.30$$

Using the same values as Example 1.2:

$$AUD/USD = 1.0237$$
$$\text{Pip value} = AUD\ 0.00009768 \text{ or } USD\ 0.0001$$
$$\text{Pip value for standard lot} = USD\ 0.0001 \times 100{,}000$$
$$= USD\ 10$$

Mini Lot

If you trade mini lots instead, the value of 1 pip will decrease by a factor of 10. Using the same values as Example 1.1:

$$USD/CHF = 0.9235$$
$$\text{Pip value} = USD\ 0.000108$$
$$\text{Pip value for mini lot} = USD\ 0.000108 \times 10{,}000$$
$$= USD\ 1.08$$

Looking at the USD/JPY example with quotes to two decimal places:

$$USD/JPY = 81.55$$
$$\text{Pip value} = USD\ 0.000123$$
$$\text{Pip value for mini lot} = USD\ 0.000123 \times 10{,}000$$
$$= USD\ 1.23$$

Using the same values as Example 1.2:

$$AUD/USD = 1.0237$$
$$\text{Pip value} = AUD\ 0.00009768 \text{ or } USD\ 0.0001$$
$$\text{Pip value for mini lot} = USD\ 0.0001 \times 10{,}000$$
$$= USD\ 1$$

LEVERAGE

Financial success is almost always accomplished through the use of leverage. I sum up the definition of leverage in four simple words: "Doing more with less."

In the previous section, we talked about how the value of 1 pip dramatically increases when a trader trades a standard lot or even a mini lot.

In reality, not many retail traders are able to fork out $100,000 or $10,000 to trade one standard or one mini lot.

This is where the forex broker steps in. Simply put, the business model of forex brokers is to provide retail traders with leverage so that they do not need to lay out the entire sum of $100,000 to trade one standard lot.

Let's see how this works. If the broker provides you with leverage of 100:1, instead of $100,000, all you need to do is to pay $1,000 to trade one standard lot. Sometimes the $1,000 is referred to as margin. It is also the basis of how brokers refer to our trading account as a margin account.

Margin basically allows a trader to purchase a contract without the need to provide the full value of the contract. In the example, $1,000 was the margin required for you to trade $100,000 on a leverage of 100:1.

Using a simple formula:

$$\text{Margin required} = \text{Lot size}/\text{Leverage}$$

Hence, for the example:

$$\text{Margin required} = \$100,000/100$$
$$= \$1,000$$

$$\text{Margin percentage} = \text{Margin amount}/\text{Lot size}$$
$$= \$1,000/\$100,000$$
$$= 1\%$$

Similarly, if the broker provides you with leverage of 50:1, instead of $100,000, all you need to do is to lay out $2,000 to trade one standard lot. Margin percentage in this case is then 2%.

In summary, the higher the leverage provided by the broker, the less you need to pay out to trade one standard lot.

Table 1.2 summarizes the leverage and subsequent margin requirements when you trade.

TABLE 1.2 Margin and Leverage

Margin Required	Maximum Leverage
5%	20:1
3%	33:1
2%	50:1
1%	100:1
0.5%	200:1
0.2%	500:1

From the table, it would be logical for us to conclude that we should choose the highest leverage available, since that would require us to pay out the least amount of cash to trade one standard lot.

This is not true.

Risk of Excessive Leverage

Leverage is a double-edged sword. While it has the potential to magnify a trader's gains, it certainly has the potential to magnify losses as well. In fact, the greater the leverage, the greater the risk.

Let's take a look at an example.

Both Trader A and Trader B open an account with a broker and start trading with a capital of USD10,000. Trader A uses leverage of 100:1 while Trader B uses leverage of 10:1. Both traders then decide to sell EUR/USD because the ongoing sovereign debt crisis is putting some pressure on the euro.

Trader A's total contract size is $100 \times \$10,000 = 1$ million. This equals to 10 standard lots. Trader B's total contract size is $10 \times \$10,000 = \$100,000$. This equals to 1 standard lot.

For EUR/USD, we learned that 1 pip equals USD10 for one standard lot.

If the trade goes against them by 50 pips, both traders will incur these losses:

Trader A: (10 lots) $\times$ (50 pips) $\times$ ($10/pip) = USD5,000

Trader B: (1 lot) $\times$ (50 pips) $\times$ ($10/pip) = USD500

The USD5,000 loss represents 50% of Trader A's trading capital, but the USD500 loss represents just 5% of Trader B's trading capital.

Take a look at Table 1.3 for the summary of two traders who trade with different leverage.

In conclusion, while leverage has the potential to magnify your profits, it also has the power to amplify your losses. It cuts both ways. After the

TABLE 1.3 Trading with Different Leverage (USD)

	Trader A	Trader B
Trading capital	$10,000	$10,000
Leverage used	100 times	10 times
Total value of transaction	$1 million	$100,000
50 pip loss	−$5,000	−$500
% loss of trading capital	50%	5%
% of trading capital remaining	50%	95%

global financial crisis of 2008 to 2010, U.S. regulators moved to regulate the forex industry there. On October 18, 2010, the National Futures Association passed rules to limit the amount of leverage retail forex brokers can provide. The rules limited leverage to 50:1 on major currencies and only 20:1 on minor currencies.

SUMMARY

The forex market is the largest financial market in the world, trading in excess of USD4 trillion in a single day. Although hundreds of currencies change hands every day, most of the trading centers on seven major currency pairs. The currency pair that handles the highest volume of trade is the EUR/USD.

A forex quote is always displayed in pairs. Examples include EUR/USD, USD/JPY, and AUD/CHF. The currency on the left is called the base currency while the currency on the right is called the counter currency. Almost all currency pairs are quoted to four decimal places, except when the Japanese yen appears in the counter currency. In such cases, the forex quote is displayed in two decimal places.

A pip is the smallest price movement in a currency pair. If the EUR/USD moves up from 1.3435 to 1.3436, this movement is called 1 pip. Similarly, if the same quote moves down from 1.3435 to 1.3434, the movement is also called 1 pip. Whenever the U.S. dollar appears as a counter currency, 1 pip earns the trader USD10 for one standard lot.

Some forex brokers go one step further and quote prices to five decimal places. For such brokers, the EUR/USD quote could be seen as 1.34358. It is important for us to take note that the fifth decimal place is not called a pip but a pipette. Quotes that have the Japanese yen as the counter currency are displayed in three decimal places instead of two in these cases.

Brokers provide retail traders with leverage to trade the forex market. Without leverage, a trader would need to pay out USD100,000 to trade one standard lot of currencies. With a 100:1 leverage, a trader would need to put up only 1/100th of the entire amount, or USD1,000. This amount is called margin. Margin basically allows a trader to purchase a contract without the need to provide the full value of the contract.

The higher the leverage employed, the smaller the margin required to trade one standard lot. Some brokers even offer leverage up to 500:1. This means traders need only USD200 to control USD100,000 worth of currencies.

Leverage is a double-edged sword. Although it helps to magnify a trader's gains, it can also amplify a trader's losses. Hence, it is imperative that traders fully understand the pros and cons of leverage before deciding the appropriate amount of leverage to employ.

CHAPTER 2

How Money Is Made in the Game

This chapter starts with an explanation of how currencies are bought or sold in the market. We then decode a forex contract for long and short. The chapter also explains the three critical points in every trade and points out the bid/ask spread that brokers charge for each trade. This chapter also presents the four reasons that cause currencies to fluctuate on a daily basis. We then turn to the fraction theory, which helps us to decide on a long or short trade. The chapter ends with an explanation of how charts are read and how market structure is identified.

BUY LOW, SELL HIGH

Forex traders make money by speculating on the movement of currency rates. There are only two ways to do this. The first way is to buy, expecting prices to rise. The second way is to sell, expecting prices to fall.

Buy

The current rate for AUD/USD is now 1.0325. You enter into a buy position because you expect the Australian dollar to strengthen further against the U.S. dollar. A buy trade is termed a "long position" in the forex market.

After three hours, the AUD/USD rate is at 1.0375. You were right, and you made 50 pips on this trade. Another way of saying this is that your long position took profit. Let's have a look at Example 2.1 for an exact contract.

EXAMPLE 2.1: BUY AUD/USD AT 1.0325

Let's assume that you buy 100,000 Australian dollars for this contract, or one standard lot. Since the exchange rate is 1.0325, you pay AUD100,000 with USD103,250.

After three hours, the AUD/USD rate goes up to 1.0375. You then sell the AUD100,000 and receive USD103,750. This transaction nets you a total profit of USD500.

Action	AUD	USD
Buy AUD100,000 at the current AUD/USD rate of 1.0325.	+ 100,000	− 103,250
3 hours later, sell AUD100,000 at the rate of 1.0375.	− 100,000	+ 103,750
Total profit earned USD **500**	0	+ 500

If you did not use leverage, you had to fork out USD103,250 to make USD500. Percentage-wise, your return is only 0.484% (500/103,250).

However, if you utilized leverage of 100:1 provided by the broker, you would only have needed to lay out margin of USD1,032.50 to buy AUD100,000. Percentage-wise, your return would have been a whopping 48.4% (500/1,032.50).

Sell

The current rate for EUR/USD is at 1.3142. You enter into a sell position because you expect the euro to further weaken against the U.S. dollar. A sell trade is termed a "short position" in the forex market.

After two hours, the EUR/USD rate is at 1.3112. You were right, and you made 30 pips on this trade. Another way of saying this is that your short position took profit. Let's have a look at Example 2.2 for an exact contract.

EXAMPLE 2.2: SELL EUR/USD AT 1.3142

Let's assume that you sell 200,000 euros for this contract, or two standard lots. Since the exchange rate is 1.3142, you receive USD262,840 for 200,000 euros. After two hours, the EUR/USD rate goes down to 1.3112.

You then buy back the 200,000 euros and pay USD262,240. This transaction nets you a total profit of USD600.

Action	EUR	USD
Sell 200,000 euros at the current EUR/USD rate of 1.3142.	− 200,000	+ 262,800
2 hours later, buy back 200,000 euros at the rate of 1.3112.	+ 200,000	− 262,240
Total profit earned USD **600**	0	+ 600

Similarly, If no leverage was employed, you had to utilize 200,000 euros, or USD262,840, to make USD600. Percentage-wise, this represents a return of only 0.228% (600/262,840).

However, if you utilized leverage of 100:1 provided by the broker, you would only have needed to lay out margin of USD2,628.40 to sell 200,000 euros. Percentage-wise, your return would have been a whopping 22.8% (600/2,628.40).

THREE POINTS IN EVERY TRADE

When you execute a position, there are essentially three points in every trade: entry price, profit target, and stop loss.

The entry price is defined as the price at which a trade is triggered. The profit target is defined as the price where the trade exits with a profit. The stop loss is defined as the price where the trade exits with a loss.

Let's use an example for both a long and a short position.

Long Position

Let's take the current GBP/USD price as 1.5743. Because you expect the pound to appreciate against the U.S. dollar, you enter into a long position.

You decide to take a profit of 30 pips and a stop loss of 30 pips. Once these values are locked down in the broker's platform, only two things can happen: The trade will hit either the profit target or the stop loss.

In this example:

Entry price = 1.5743

Stop loss = 1.5713

Profit target = 1.5773

Figure 2.1 reflects this trade.

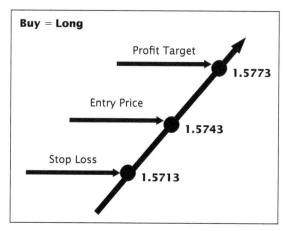

FIGURE 2.1   Concept of a Long Trade

FIGURE 2.2   Enter for Long Position

For a long position, the profit target is located above the entry price while the stop loss is located below the entry price. In this example, you take an equal amount of pips for the exit: 30 pips above the entry price and 30 pips below the entry price.

Whenever a trade reflects an equal distance between the entry price to the profit target and between the entry price to the stop loss, the trade is said to have a risk to reward ratio of 1:1. Figures 2.2 and 2.3 show an actual progression of a long trade that took profit.

FIGURE 2.3 Exit with a Profit

Source: Created with FX Primus Ltd, a PRIME Mantle Corporation PLC company.

Figures 2.4 and 2.5 show an actual progression of a long trade that hit a stop loss.

FIGURE 2.4 Enter for Long Position

Source: Created with FX Primus Ltd, a PRIME Mantle Corporation PLC company.

FIGURE 2.5   Exit with a Stop Loss

Short Position

Let's take the current NZD/USD price as 0.8138. You expect the New Zealand dollar to fall against the U.S. dollar; hence, you enter into a short position.

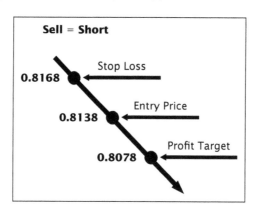

FIGURE 2.6   Concept of a Short Trade

You decide to take a profit of 60 pips and a stop loss of 30 pips. Once these values are locked down in the broker's platform, only two things can happen: The trade will hit either the profit target or the stop loss.

In this example:

Entry price = 0.8138

Stop loss = 0.8168

Profit target = 0.8078

Figure 2.6 reflects this trade.

For a short position, the profit target is located below the entry price while the stop loss is located above the entry price. In this example, you set a 30 pip stop loss but a profit target of 60 pips. This is termed a 1:2 risk to reward ratio.

Figures 2.7 and 2.8 show an actual progression of a short trade that took profit.

Figures 2.9 and 2.10 show an actual progression of a short trade that hit a stop loss.

FIGURE 2.7 Enter for a Short

FIGURE 2.8 Exit with a Profit

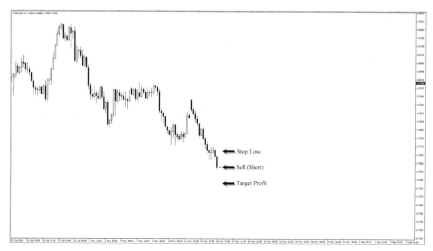

FIGURE 2.9 Enter for a Short

Source: Created with FX Primus Ltd, a PRIME Mantle Corporation PLC company.
All rights reserved.

FIGURE 2.10 Exit with a Loss

Source: Created with FX Primus Ltd, a PRIME Mantle Corporation PLC company.
All rights reserved.

The greatest lesson in this segment is this: Always put a stop loss for every trade. To most traders, having a profit target is second nature, but hardly anyone thinks about putting a stop loss. The purpose of a stop loss is simple yet critical. It is essentially a level that tells you to exit the trade with an acceptable loss because the trade is not going your way.

Far too many times in my career as a trader and coach, I have seen countless traders blow up their accounts simply because they refuse to put a stop loss for every trade. When it comes to trading the forex market, we will never be right all the time. The purpose of a stop loss is to help us, not harm us.

Traders run the risk of blowing up their entire account by leaving a trade "naked," or without a stop loss. Do not adopt this practice. Interestingly enough, the same group of traders who blow up their accounts by not placing a stop loss is the same group who walks away from the forex market thinking that it's risky.

BID/ASK SPREAD

So far, we have been talking about forex prices as a single quote. In reality, there are actually two quotes for each price: the bid price and the ask price. The bid price is the price at which the trader selects to sell. It is also the price at which the broker is willing to buy.

The ask price is the price at which the trader selects to buy. It is also the price at which the broker is willing to sell. The difference between the bid price and the ask price is known as the *spread*. The spread is the transaction fee that the broker charges for executing a trade.

In Figure 2.11, the EUR/USD quote is given as 1.3089/1.3091.

This figure tells us that the bid price is 1.3089 and the ask price is 1.3091. We can also infer that the spread is 2 pips. This means that the broker FXPRIMUS charges a transaction fee of 2 pips for every trade that is executed on its platform.

If you believe that the EUR/USD will rise, you would click "Buy," and the trade will be triggered on the ask price of 1.3091. If you believe that the EUR/USD will fall, you would click "Sell," and the trade will be triggered on the bid price of 1.3089.

There are three important facts for us to take note when it comes to spread:

1. The spread is the only transaction fee incurred when trading on the broker's platform.

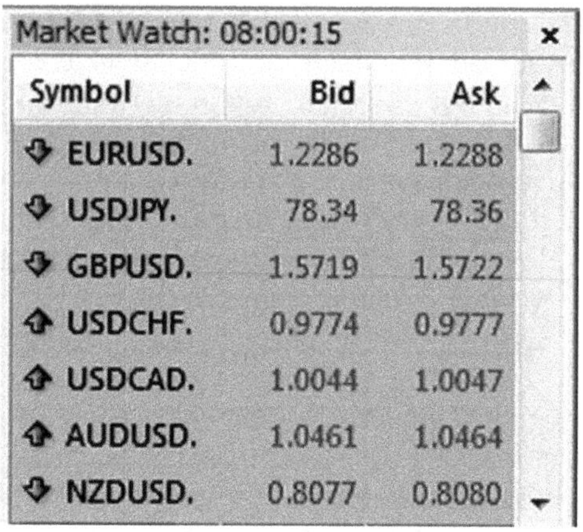

Market Watch: 08:00:15			✕
Symbol	**Bid**	**Ask**	▲
⬇ EURUSD.	1.2286	1.2288	
⬇ USDJPY.	78.34	78.36	
⬇ GBPUSD.	1.5719	1.5722	
⬆ USDCHF.	0.9774	0.9777	
⬆ USDCAD.	1.0044	1.0047	
⬆ AUDUSD.	1.0461	1.0464	
⬇ NZDUSD.	0.8077	0.8080	▼

FIGURE 2.11 EUR/USD Quote on FXPRIMUS Market Watch

2. The spread is charged for every "round turn." This means that only 2 pips are charged for a complete transaction of buying first and selling later or selling first and buying later.

3. The smaller the spread, the less the market needs to move in your favor to register a profit.

Typically, spreads on more liquid pairs are smaller, with illiquid pairs reflecting higher spreads. Since every forex quote is accompanied by both the bid and the ask price, when you execute a buy or long position, you enter on the ask price and exit on the bid price.

Figure 2.12 shows an example. To earn 30 pips, the market has to move 32 pips.

With a spread of 2 pips on the EUR/USD, a long position is executed on the ask price of 1.3127. To make 30 pips profit, the market has to move 32 pips to cover the pip spread that is paid to the broker. The long position is then exited on the bid price of 1.3157.

Similarly, when you execute a sell or short position, you enter on the bid price and exit on the ask price. Figure 2.13 shows an example. To earn 30 pips, the market has to move 33 pips.

With a spread of 3 pips on the GBP/USD, a short position is executed on the bid price of 1.5968. To make 30 pips profit, the market has to move 33 pips to cover the pip spread that is paid to the broker. The short position is then exited on the ask price of 1.5938.

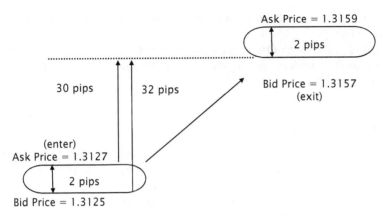

FIGURE 2.12 Long Position on EUR/USD

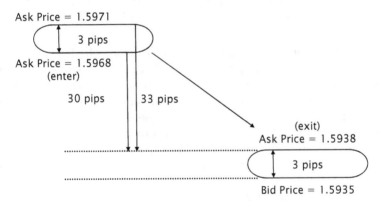

FIGURE 2.13 Short Position on GBP/USD

Now that we have a better understanding of how money is made on the forex market, let's take a look at reasons that cause currency pairs to move up and down.

WHAT CAUSES THE PRICE OF CURRENCIES TO FLUCTUATE?

The value of a currency rises or falls in relation to the forces of demand and supply. When the demand for a currency exceeds the available supply, the value of the currency tends to rise. Conversely, when the supply of a currency exceeds the available demand, the value of the currency tends to fall.

Let's look at four of the most important factors that cause prices of currencies to fluctuate: economic factors, political factors, natural disasters, and speculation.

Economic Factors

When traders look at economic factors, they are searching for one key word: growth. When growth is non-existent or negative, the value of the country's currency tends to fall. This is because the currency is not viewed as attractive or valuable, and traders start selling it.

Conversely, when growth is positive, the value of the country's currency tends to rise. This is because more traders end up buying the currency. Traders look at several economic factors to gain an idea of how a country is performing. Let's take a look at a couple of them.

Consumer Spending   Everyone needs to spend, whether on goods or services. Consumer spending directly affects the money supply of a country, which directly affects the country's currency and subsequent exchange rate with other nations. When consumer spending increases, the general health of the economy increases, and subsequent demand for the country's currency will lift its value against other currencies.

On the flip side, when consumer spending declines, the economy falters and the general sentiment of the currency turns bad. This causes the country's currency to fall against other currencies.

As shown in this report:

> *"The pound rose for a second day versus the dollar after the government's quarterly economic growth report showed consumer spending rose more than forecast, boosting speculation the country will avoid a recession."*

> *Bloomberg Businessweek,* February 24, 2012

Current Account Balance   The current account balance is a measure of how much money is flowing out of the country compared with how much is flowing in from foreign sources. If there is a net inflow of funds, the country is said to have a current account surplus. If there is a net outflow of funds, the country is said to have a current account deficit.

Continuous records of current account deficits may lead to a natural depreciation of a country's currency. This is because money for trade, income, and aid is leaving the country to make payments in a foreign currency. The current account is made up of three components:

Current account = Trade balance + Net income + Unilateral transfers

The trade balance is simply the total value of exports minus the total value of imports. Net income is defined as the difference between money received and money paid out. It includes salaries, interest payments, and dividends. Unilateral transfers include taxes, foreign aid, and one-way gifts.

For most countries, the largest component of the current account is generally the trade balance. As an example, the United States has experienced high current account deficits for the last few decades primarily because of its large trade deficit.

As shown in this report:

"The yen weakened after official data showed Japan had a record current account deficit in January. The yen slid 0.3 percent to 81.33 per dollar as of 8:53 am in Tokyo. It declined 0.2 percent to 106.85 per euro."

Bloomberg Businessweek, March 8, 2012

In Chapter 7, we will discuss more specific economic news that affects the currency market and how to trade such news for profit.

Political Factors

When a country is mired in a political crisis, demand for its goods and services is affected. These problems would cause foreign capital coming into the country to cease and also cause foreign capital to leave the country. The combined effect leaves the home currency weaker against other currencies.

An upcoming election can also have a big impact on a country's currency. Traders typically view elections as events that give rise to potential political instability and uncertainty, which equates to greater volatility in the currency.

This effect is more strongly felt when governments change hands. A new government often signifies a change in ideology and management, which translates to new rules, new laws, and new policies that ultimately will affect the value of the currency.

The change in the currency value could be either positive or negative. Political parties that make a stand on promoting economic growth and reining in high government debt levels tend to boost a currency's value.

As shown in this report:

> *"Egypt's pound fell on Wednesday to its lowest level against the U.S. dollar since January 2005 after the biggest anti-government protests of President Hosni Mubarak's three-decade rule. The pound fell as low as 5.830 against the U.S. currency."*

Reuters, January 26, 2011

Natural Disasters

Natural disasters, such as earthquakes, tornadoes, and floods, can bring about devastating effects to a country. Loss of life, damaged infrastructure, and abrupt changes to daily living all have a negative impact on the nation's currency.

Economic output will also be severely affected because of the damage caused. Money that could have otherwise been used to drive economic initiatives is now channeled towards rebuilding supply chains and infrastructure.

The problem is further compounded by a decrease in consumer spending and loss of consumer and investor confidence. Ironically, other nations may benefit from the tragedy because of a jump in import orders from the disaster-stricken nation. All of these factors combined take a toll on the currency of the nation.

As shown in these reports:

> *"Australia's currency fell to the lowest level as confidence about growth prospects for the country waned in the wake of heavy flooding in the state of Queensland. The AUDUSD fell 0.5% to buy 99.60 U.S. cents, adding to a loss of 2.5% this week."*

Market Watch, January 6, 2012

> *"The New Zealand dollar declined in the Asian session on Tuesday after Christchurch, New Zealand's second-largest city was struck by a strong earthquake. NZD/USD fell from 0.7634 to 0.7550 extending its losses further to just below 0.7500. NZD/USD's level of 0.74 was last seen on December 28, 2012."*

RTTNews, December 22, 2011

"Indonesia's rupiah fell to its lowest level in almost three weeks after northwestern Indonesia was hit by a magnitude 8.7 earthquake. Indonesia's rupiah weakened 0.2 percent to 9,205 per dollar after strengthening 0.4 percent before the quake. It touched 9,208, the weakest level since March 23."

Bloomberg Businessweek, April 11, 2012

Speculation

Speculators trade the forex market purely for profit. There are basically two categories of speculators in the market: retail traders and hedge funds. On average, more than 90% of the daily trading volume in the forex market is speculative in nature.

Speculative moves are sometimes called "smart money" or "hot money" because these moves are the first to move in and out of countries. As an example, if speculators believe that a country's economy has expanded too much and is in danger of overheating, they may get out of the currency in anticipation of cooling measures by the government. This would cause more supply than demand for the currency, causing it to depreciate.

One of the world's most remembered speculative plays on the forex market happened on September 16, 1992, also known as Black Wednesday. On that fateful day, currency speculator George Soros bet heavily against the pound and made USD1 billion in the process. Two weeks prior to Black Wednesday, currency speculators, including Soros, sold billions of pounds, hoping to buy them back cheaply and profit on the difference.

The British government decided to intervene by hiking interests rates to 12%. The Treasury also tried to prop up the pound by spending £27 billion of reserves. However, the government measures were all but futile.

On the evening of September 16, the British Conservative government announced its exit from the European exchange rate mechanism (ERM), conceding defeat that it could not hold the British pound/ Deutsche mark floor of 2.778. Within a few hours of the announcement, the pound tumbled 3% and was down more than 12% within three weeks. In 1997, the UK Treasury estimated the cost of Black Wednesday to be GBP3.4 billion.

FRACTION THEORY

Let's now take a look at the fraction theory, which helps us ascertain long or short trades. Let's take a look at the EUR/USD currency pair. Instead of writing it in the normal quote of EUR/USD, we write it in the form of a fraction like this:

$$\frac{EUR}{USD}$$

In this fraction, the euro is the numerator while the U.S. dollar is the denominator. If the numerator becomes bigger while the denominator keeps constant, the entire fraction becomes bigger. This means that if the euro strengthens for whatever reason, the EUR/USD currency pair will head higher. The euro can strengthen for a variety of reasons, and we discuss some of the scenarios throughout the book.

Similarly, if the denominator becomes bigger while the numerator keeps constant, the entire fraction becomes smaller. This means that if the U.S. dollar strengthens for whatever reason, the EUR/USD currency pair will head lower. The crux of the fraction theory is in pairing the strongest currency against the weakest currency at any point of time.

If we pair the strongest currency in the numerator against the weakest currency in the denominator, we get a strong uptrend. Our job in this case is to go long. If we pair the weakest currency in the numerator against the strongest currency in the denominator, we get a strong downtrend. Our job in this case is to go short.

Here's an example of a strong/weak pairing:

On April 3, 2012, Federal Reserve policy makers announced that they would consider additional stimulus only if the economy lost momentum or if inflation stayed below the 2% target. This contrasted with their January meeting minutes, in which some policy makers saw the economy requiring additional action "before long." The Federal Open Market Committee minutes were more hawkish than expected and caught the market by surprise, which strengthened the U.S. dollar.

On the same day, Spain held its bond auction program. The auction proved to be a huge disappointment as Spain managed to sell only 2.69 billion euros out of a maximum target of 3.5 billion euros. Additionally, Spanish credit-default swaps widened out to 450 basis points—the highest reading in three months. This event weakened the euro.

Using fraction theory to explain these events, we can say that the euro weakened because of Spain's disappointing bond auction and the U.S. dollar strengthened because of the hawkish stance by the Federal Reserve. This combined action caused the EUR/USD to plummet, free-falling 300 pips in one day (see Figure 2.14).

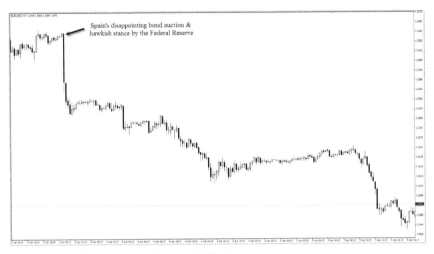

Spain's disappointing bond auction & hawkish stance by the Federal Reserve

FIGURE 2.14 EUR/USD Plummets 300 Pips

READING THE CHARTS

There are three types of charts which traders use on the broker's platform. The three charts include line chart, bar chart, and candlestick chart.

Line Chart

The line chart is plotted by connecting the closing prices over a specific time frame. With a simple line, the price trend of a particular currency can be seen. The line chart is applicable for all currency pairs, across all time frames. As a trader, it is important to select the time frame that you are comfortable with. A short time frame can help you to spot minor trends for quick profits, while a longer time frame can help you to align yourself with the dominant trend.

The simplicity of the line chart comes with one glaring drawback: Because all the line ever records is the closing price, traders are not able to see any drastic moves prior to the close of the period. Hence, traders are not able to utilize vital market information to aid their decision-making process.

Figure 2.15 presents a line chart for USD/CAD using the 5-minute time frame.

Figure 2.16 presents a line chart for USD/CAD using the hourly time frame.

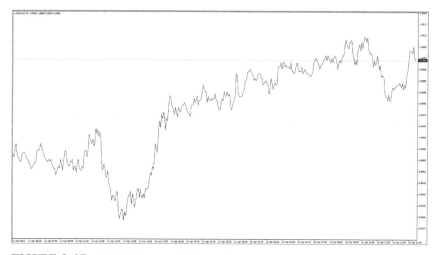

FIGURE 2.15 USD/CAD on a 5-Minute Time Frame

Source: Created with FX Primus Ltd, a PRIME Mantle Corporation PLC company.

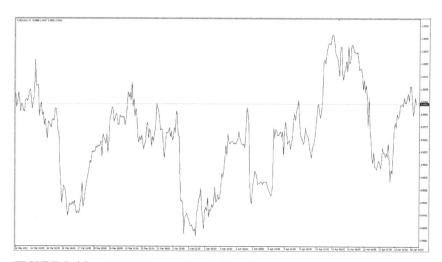

FIGURE 2.16 USD/CAD on an Hourly Time Frame

Source: Created with FX Primus Ltd, a PRIME Mantle Corporation PLC company.

Bar Chart

A bar chart gives slightly more information than a line chart because it records the open, high, low, and close of the market price for the currency pair. Unlike the line chart, which gives data at only one point in time, the bar chart offers more data about the price changes during the selected time frame. Bar charts are sometimes referred to as OHLC charts, because they capture the price for open, high, low, and close.

Figure 2.17 shows an example of a price bar.

The OHLC readings on bar charts are:

OPEN: The horizontal line on the left stands for the opening price of the currency pair in a selected time period.

HIGH: The top point of the vertical line shows the highest price of the currency pair during that time period.

LOW: The bottom point of the vertical line shows the lowest price of the currency pair during that time period.

CLOSE: The horizontal line on the right shows the closing price of the currency pair in the selected time period.

The individual vertical bars in the chart (low and high) indicate the currency pair's trading range as a whole. Depending on the time frame selected, bar charts can summarize price activity over the past minute, hour, day, or even month.

Figure 2.18 shows the bar chart for USD/JPY in a 15-minute time frame. Figure 2.19 shows the bar chart for AUD/USD in a 4-hour time frame.

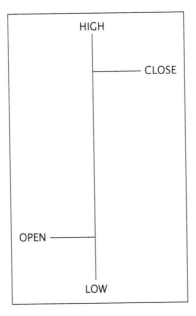

FIGURE 2.17 Price Bar

FIGURE 2.18   USD/JPY in a 15-Minute Time Frame

Source: Created with FX Primus Ltd, a PRIME Mantle Corporation PLC company.

FIGURE 2.19   AUD/USD in a 4-Hour Time Frame

Source: Created with FX Primus Ltd, a PRIME Mantle Corporation PLC company.

Candlestick Chart

Candlestick charts were invented by the Japanese in the 1700s to study the movements in the price of rice on Japanese commodity exchanges. Candlestick charts show the same information as bar charts but in a more visually appealing way.

Take a look at the two candlesticks in Figure 2.20.

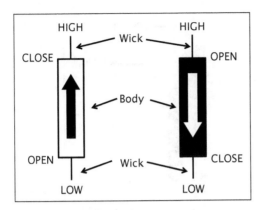

FIGURE 2.20 Bull and Bear Candlesticks

The OHLC readings are the same as with bar charts. Please see the explanatory note before Figure 2.17 for a definition of each reading.

A candlestick is considered bullish if the closing price is higher than the opening price. A candlestick is considered bearish if the closing price is lower than the opening price. In Figure 2.20, the candlestick on the left is considered bullish and the one on the right is considered bearish.

The "real body" of the candlestick represents the range between the opening price and the closing price for a particular time frame. Real bodies can be either long or short.

The "wicks," or shadows, above and below the candlestick represent the highest and lowest prices reached during a particular time frame. Shadows can be long or short.

Figure 2.21 shows a bullish candlestick on the 30-minute (M30) time frame for the EUR/USD currency pair.

Here's how we would interpret the candlestick, assuming that the candle started forming at 11 A.M.: At 11 A.M., the price for EUR/USD was 1.3340. At 11:30 A.M., the price for EUR/USD closed higher at 1.3365. In the half-hour period, prices fluctuated such that the highest price reached was 1.3378 and the lowest price reached was 1.3322.

Figure 2.22 shows a bearish candlestick on the 4-hour (H4) time frame for the USD/JPY currency pair.

Here's how we would interpret the candlestick, assuming that the candle started forming at 2 P.M.: At 2 P.M., the price for USD/JPY was 81.78. At 6 P.M., the price for USD/JPY closed lower at 81.02. In the 4-hour period, prices fluctuated such that the highest price reached was 81.92 and the lowest price reached was 80.87.

In summary, reading candlesticks can give us an idea of which group—buyers or sellers—was in control at any point of time.

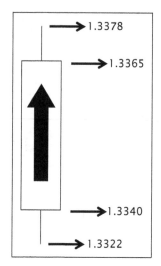

FIGURE 2.21 Bullish Candlestick

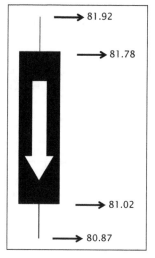

FIGURE 2.22 Bearish Candlestick

MARKET STRUCTURE

Now that we understand how to read the candlesticks, let's turn to market structure. The forex market has three segments: trend, range, and breakout.

Trend

A trend can go either up or down. A trend that is moving upwards is called an uptrend. A trend that is moving downwards is called a downtrend.

Uptrend   An uptrend is identified as prices having a series of higher highs and higher lows. The highs are the peaks that prices reach intermittently. The lows are the valleys that prices fall to before heading up again. Hence, an uptrend is formed when there is a series of highs going higher and a series of lows going higher.

Figure 2.23 shows an example of an uptrend.

Figure 2.24 shows an example of EUR/USD (1-hour time frame) moving in an uptrend.

Figure 2.25 shows an example of USD/JPY (4-hour time frame) moving in an uptrend.

FIGURE 2.23   Series of Higher Highs and Higher Lows

FIGURE 2.24 EUR/USD Moving in an Uptrend

Source: Created with FX Primus Ltd, a PRIME Mantle Corporation PLC company.

FIGURE 2.25 USD/JPY Moving in an Uptrend

Source: Created with FX Primus Ltd, a PRIME Mantle Corporation PLC company.

Downtrend   A downtrend has prices moving in a series of lower highs and lower lows. (See Figure 2.26.)

Figure 2.27 shows an example of USD/JPY (1-hour time frame) moving in a downtrend.

Figure 2.28 shows an example of EUR/AUD (4-hour time frame) moving in a downtrend.

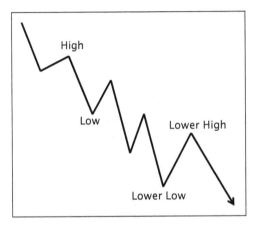

FIGURE 2.26   Series of Lower Lows and Lower Highs

FIGURE 2.27   USD/JPY Moving in a Downtrend

FIGURE 2.28   EUR/AUD Moving in a Downtrend

Source: Created with FX Primus Ltd, a PRIME Mantle Corporation PLC company.
All rights reserved.

Traders use a trending strategy when the market is moving in an uptrend or a downtrend. When the market is in an uptrend, we would go long. If the market is moving in a downtrend, we would go short.

Trend Lines   Trend lines are lines that are drawn to show the prevailing direction of price. They are visual representations to give us insight into where prices could go next. In an uptrend, we draw a trend line by joining the significant higher lows. In a downtrend, we draw the trend line by joining the significant lower highs.

The steeper the angle of the trend line, the stronger the momentum. However, it is important to note that trends with steep angles are very often short-lived.

Traders use trend lines to show three things:

1. The direction of the trend
2. The angle of the trend
3. The possible chart patterns that may evolve

Figure 2.29 shows an example of an uptrend line drawn on USD/JPY (4-hour time frame)

Figure 2.30 shows an example of a downtrend line on the AUD/USD (1-hour time frame)

FIGURE 2.29 USD/JPY Moving in an Uptrend

FIGURE 2.30 AUD/USD Moving in a Downtrend

Understanding a Trend In an uptrend, it is easy for us to conclude that prices rise because there are more buyers than sellers. However, this is not true. In the forex market, the number of contracts bought always equals the number of contracts sold. As an example, if you want to buy five lots of EUR/USD, the contract must be available from someone who wants to sell it. Conversely, if you want to sell three lots of USD/CHF, someone must be willing to buy it.

Hence, the number of long and short positions in the forex market is always equal. If the number of contracts bought and sold is always equal, why do prices move up and down?

The reason lies in the intensity of emotions between the buyers and the sellers. In an uptrend, the buyers are in control because they don't mind paying a high price. They buy high because they expect prices to rise even higher. Sellers are nervous in an uptrend, and they agree to sell only at a higher price. The price moves up because the intensity of the buyers' greed overpowers the fear and anxiety of the sellers. The uptrend starts to fail only when buyers refuse to buy at higher prices anymore.

In a downtrend, the sellers are in control because they don't mind selling at a low price. They sell low because they expect prices to drop even further. Buyers are nervous in a downtrend, and they agree to buy only at a discount. The price moves down because the intensity of the sellers' greed overpowers the buyers' fear and anxiety. The downtrend starts to fail only when sellers refuse to sell at lower prices anymore.

Range

A range occurs when the price is trading in a channel between two borders. Using an analogy of a bouncing rubber ball, the price seems to "bounce" between a floor and a ceiling. The ceiling is called an area of resistance while the floor is called an area of support. (See Figure 2.31.)

Figure 2.32 shows an example of GBP/JPY (30-minute time frame) moving in a range.

Figure 2.33 shows an example of EUR/JPY (daily time frame) moving in a range.

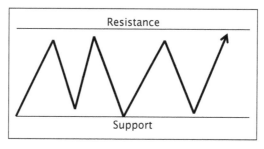

FIGURE 2.31 Concept of a Range

FIGURE 2.32   GBP/JPY Moving in a Range

Source: Created with FX Primus Ltd, a PRIME Mantle Corporation PLC company.

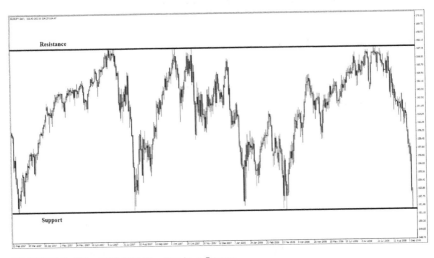

FIGURE 2.33   EUR/JPY Moving in a Range

Source: Created with FX Primus Ltd, a PRIME Mantle Corporation PLC company.

In a range, traders go short once prices bounce off levels of resistance because prices tend to head downwards. Similarly, traders execute long orders once prices bounce off levels of support because prices tend to head upwards.

Figure 2.34 shows an example of where traders place buy and sell orders in a range.

Figure 2.35 shows an example of where traders place buy and sell orders on the GBP/JPY (30-minute time frame).

Figure 2.36 shows an example of where traders place buy and sell orders on the EUR/JPY (daily time frame).

Breakout

A breakout occurs when prices push above the resistance area or below the support area after bouncing between a trading channel for a period

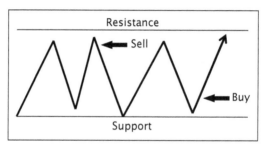

FIGURE 2.34   Concept of a Range

FIGURE 2.35   GBP/JPY Moving in a Range

Source: Created with FX Primus Ltd, a PRIME Mantle Corporation PLC company.
All rights reserved.

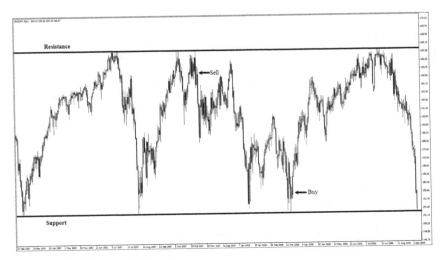

FIGURE 2.36 EUR/JPY in a Range

Source: Created with FX Primus Ltd, a PRIME Mantle Corporation PLC company. All rights reserved.

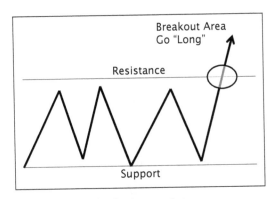

FIGURE 2.37 Breakout from the Resistance Area

of time. Momentum is greatest on breakout points; hence traders tend to capitalize on these specific movements by going long once prices break upward from a trading range or by going short once prices break downward from a trading range.

Figure 2.37 shows an example of a breakout from the resistance area.

Figure 2.38 shows an example of a breakout on USD/JPY (1-hour time frame).

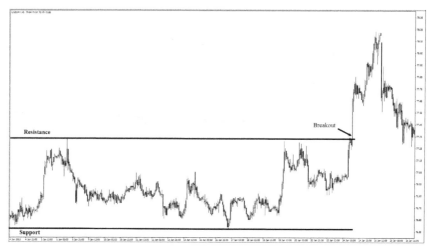

FIGURE 2.38   USD/JPY Breakout

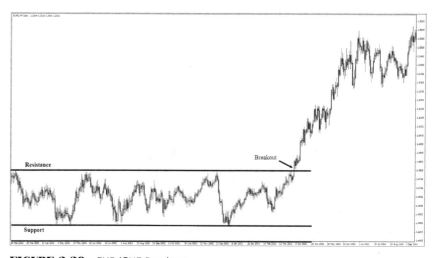

FIGURE 2.39   EUR/CHF Breakout

Figure 2.39 shows an example of a breakout on EUR/CHF (daily time frame).

Figure 2.40 shows an example of a breakout from the support area.

Figure 2.41 shows an example of a breakout on NZD/USD (1-hour time frame).

Figure 2.42 shows an example of a breakout on GBP/USD (4-hour time frame).

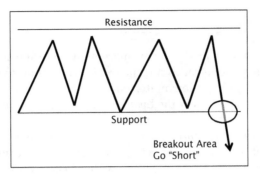

FIGURE 2.40 Breakout from the Support Area

FIGURE 2.41 NZD/USD Breakout

FIGURE 2.42 GBP/USD Breakout

SUMMARY

Traders make money in the forex market by entering long and short trades. Traders go long on a currency pair when they expect the base currency to rise against the counter currency. Traders go short on a currency pair when they expect the base currency to fall against the counter currency.

There are essentially three points in every trade: entry price, stop loss, and profit target. The entry price is the price at which the trade is triggered. The stop loss is a level to cut the trade with a loss when it doesn't go the intended way. The profit target is a level to exit the trade with a profit when the market moves the intended way.

For a long position, the profit target is located above the entry price, and the stop loss is placed below it. For a short position, the profit target is located below the entry price, and the stop loss is placed above it.

Brokers charge a fee for every long or short trade executed on their platform. This is termed the spread. In general, spreads are lower for the most liquid pairs, such as EUR/USD and USD/JPY. For long positions, traders would execute on the ask price and exit on the bid price. For short positions, traders would execute on the bid price and exit on the ask price.

Four main factors cause forex prices to fluctuate: economic factors, political factors, natural disasters, and speculation. Since currencies are quoted in pairs, the fraction theory helps traders to get a sense of the market's general direction.

The main crux of the fraction theory is to pair the strongest currency against the weakest currency at any point. If we pair the strongest currency in the numerator against the weakest currency in the denominator, the result will be a strong uptrend. In such cases, it is prudent for traders to go long. If we pair the weakest currency in the numerator against the strongest currency in the denominator, the result will be a strong downtrend. In such cases, it is prudent for traders to go short.

The three most popular ways to read a forex chart are: line chart, bar chart, and candlestick chart. The candlestick chart is the most popular choice of traders worldwide for two reasons. First, the candlestick shows the four most important price points at any given period: the open, high, low, and close prices. Second, it shows the intensity of the fight between the bulls and the bears. This is characterized by the heights of the shadows (the highs and lows) and the lengths of the candlestick bodies.

The forex market can be broken down into three simple structures: trend, range, and breakout. An uptrend occurs when prices move in a consistent fashion of higher highs and higher lows. A downtrend occurs when prices move in a consistent fashion of lower highs and lower lows.

A range occurs when prices tend to bounce between two levels of support and resistance. A breakout occurs when prices move strongly above the level of resistance or strongly below the level of support.

CHAPTER 3

The Six Major Players

The forex market is exciting because it is made up of millions of participants. The constant buying and selling by these participants adds to the unprecedented liquidity found only in the forex market. This chapter focuses on the six biggest players in the forex market. They are:

1. Central banks
2. Commercial and investment banks
3. Multinational companies (MNCs)
4. Institutional traders
5. Retail forex brokers
6. Retail traders

We start with the central banks and the three ways in which they manage inflation. We then take a sneak peek into the banking world of proprietary trading and get a grip on the Volcker Rule. We also get to know the three biggest rogue traders in history. The segment on multinational companies (MNCs) presents two examples of how importers and exporters conduct hedging activities in the forex market to gain certainty of price. Finally, a look into the retail crowd shows us why forex brokers and high-frequency trading are exploding all over the world.

CENTRAL BANKS

The main aim of central banks is to stabilize the country's economy. They do this by monitoring one of the most important benchmarks in the economy: inflation.

Inflation is commonly defined as the rate at which prices of goods and services are rising. If the central bank does not tackle inflation swiftly, it can lead to an erosion of purchasing power.

In most countries, inflation is measured through the consumer price index (CPI). The CPI is a weighted average of prices of a basket of consumer goods and services. These consumer goods and services normally include but are not limited to housing, food, transportation, recreation, education, and medical care. A central bank controls inflation in three ways:

1. It regulates interest rates.
2. It intervenes by buying or selling currencies.
3. It regulates the reserve requirement ratio.

Let's explore all three in detail.

Regulate Interest Rates—Up

Central banks normally increase interest rates when inflation is high. In simple terms, inflation is defined as "too much money chasing too few goods, causing the price of goods to increase." If no measures are taken to curb inflation, the likely effect is a weakening of the currency. When this happens, central banks step in to raise interest rates in the hope of curbing inflation and strengthening the currency again.

How does raising interest rates help this process? When central banks increase interest rates, deposit rates and lending rates in commercial banks go up accordingly. This affects two groups of people: savers and borrowers. Higher lending rates make the money "more expensive" to borrow, thus discouraging both people and businesses to take up loans. The opposite effect is also true. Higher deposit rates encourage people and businesses to save more than they normally would.

This combined effect causes the money supply in the system to decrease, thereby countering the effects of inflation. (See Examples 3.1 and 3.2.)

EXAMPLE 3.1: PEOPLE'S BANK OF CHINA INCREASES INTEREST RATES

On July 6, 2011, the People's Bank of China (PBOC) announced a 25 basis point increase in its interest rates—its fifth such move in nine months. The main reason for the increase was China's inflation—consumer prices rose 5.5% in May from a year earlier.

As shown in this report:

> "China's central bank increased interest rates for the third time this year, making clear that taming inflation is a top priority even as the economy slows gently. Benchmark one-year lending rates will be raised 25 basis points to 6.56 percent, and benchmark one-year deposit rates will be raised 25 basis points to 3.5 percent."

> *Reuters,* July 6, 2011

EXAMPLE 3.2: CENTRAL BANK OF SRI LANKA INCREASES INTEREST RATES

On February 3, 2012, the central bank of Sri Lanka raised interest rates by 50 basis points, its first increase since 2007. The rate hike was announced to contain credit growth and inflation after the country's economy expanded the most since the 1970s.

As shown in this report:

> "Sri Lanka unexpectedly raised interest rates to contain credit growth and inflation after the economy expanded the most since at least the 1970s. The Central Bank of Sri Lanka raised the reverse repurchase rate to 9 percent from 8.5 percent and the repurchase rate to 7.5 percent from 7 percent."

> *Bloomberg Businessweek,* February 14, 2012

Regulate Interest Rates—Down

Central banks decrease interest rates to weaken its currency. This normally happens when inflation rates are low. A weak currency encourages lending and ultimately stimulates growth. When central banks decrease interest rates, deposit rates and lending rates in commercial banks go down accordingly. This affects two groups of people: savers and borrowers.

Lower lending rates make the money "cheaper" to borrow, thus encouraging both people and businesses to take up loans. The opposite effect is also true. Lower deposit rates discourage people and businesses to save more than they normally would. Hence, this combined effect will cause the money supply in the system to increase, thereby stimulating growth. (See Examples 3.3, 3.4, and 3.5.)

EXAMPLE 3.3: EUROPEAN CENTRAL BANK CUTS INTEREST RATES

On November 3, 2011, the European Central Bank (ECB) cut interest rates by a quarter point, lowering the benchmark rate from 1.5% to 1.25%. The main reason for the rate cut was new ECB president Mario Draghi's concern that the Eurozone could subside into a "mild recession."
As shown in this report:

"The European Central Bank cut interest rates for the first time in two years, as Europe is heading into a mild recession. In response the ECB cuts its key rate to 1.25% from 1.5%, less than four months after it raised the rate in an effort to battle inflation."

CNN Money, November 3, 2011

In a second move, ECB president Mario Draghi cut the benchmark rates from 1.25% to 1% on December 8, 2011. The rate cut was done to encourage banks to lend again, during the European debt crisis.
As shown in this report:

"The European Central Bank cut interest rates and announced further unorthodox measures to boost liquidity but ECB President Mario Draghi disappointed markets by stopping short of pledging more aggressive bond buying."

CNBC, December 8, 2011

EXAMPLE 3.4: RESERVE BANK OF AUSTRALIA CUTS INTEREST RATES

On November 1, 2011, the Reserve Bank of Australia cut interest rates by 25 basis points from 4.75% to 4.5%, its first cut since April 2009. The move was done to combat slowing global growth caused by the debt crisis in Europe.
As shown in this report:

"The Reserve Bank of Australia (RBA) has cut interest rates amid fears of a slowdown in the global economy. The central bank lowered its key rate to 4.5% from 4.75%, the first cut since April 2009. RBA said it was concerned about the impact of global economic growth."

BBC News, November 1, 2011

EXAMPLE 3.5: RESERVE BANK OF AUSTRALIA CUTS INTEREST RATES

On December 6, 2011, the Reserve Bank of Australia (RBA) lowered the interest rate by another 25 basis points to 4.25%. The biggest reason for the rate cut was due to China's slowing growth.

As shown in this report:

"Australia's central bank reduced its benchmark interest rate today for a second straight month as Europe's fiscal crisis threatens to slow the nation's commodity exports, sending the nation's currency lower."

Bloomberg Businessweek, December 6, 2011

Central Bank Intervention

Central banks sometimes engage in currency interventions to strengthen or weaken a country's currency. (See Examples 3.6, 3.7, and 3.8.)

EXAMPLE 3.6: BANK OF JAPAN INTERVENES

On August 4, 2011, the Bank of Japan sold 4.5 trillion yen to weaken its currency. Prior to the intervention, investors had flocked to the yen because of its reputation as a safe haven among the G10 currencies. This caused the currency to strengthen considerably.

Japan is an export-oriented country that thrives on a weak currency. The yen had risen so much so that it threatened to derail Japan's recovery from the March 11 earthquake and nuclear disaster.

As shown in this report:

"The yen fell against all 16 of its most-traded counterparts after Japan yesterday sold its currency to stem gains that threaten the nation's economic recovery."

Bloomberg Businessweek, August 4, 2011

EXAMPLE 3.7: BANK OF JAPAN INTERVENES

On October 31, 2011, Japan intervened again. Prior to the intervention, the yen reached a post-war high of 75.35 against the U.S. dollar as traders and investors continued to seek refuge from Europe's fiscal debt woes and the United States' slowdown. During this second intervention, Japan sold a record 8 trillion yen, causing the yen to plunge more than 4%. At the time, Finance Minister Jun Azumi said that the move was carried out to combat one-sided speculative moves that did not reflect the economic fundamentals of the Japanese economy.

As shown in this report:

"The dollar shot up against the yen as Japan stepped in to weaken its currency after it hit a fresh post-year high against the US. The dollar stood at 79.18 against 75.82. The move also saw the euro rise sharply to 111.20 yen from 107.29."

ChannelnewsAsia, October 31, 2011

EXAMPLE 3.8: SWISS NATIONAL BANK INTERVENES

On September 6, 2011, the Swiss National Bank (SNB) intervened in the forex market to impose a ceiling on the franc by spending 11 billion francs to buy euros. This was the first time in more than three decades that such an action was taken. In a statement, the Zurich-based bank said that it "will no longer tolerate a EUR/CHF rate below 1.20 and is prepared to buy foreign currency in unlimited quantities."

At the time, the franc had been steadily gaining against the entire basket of G8 currencies. In fact, before the intervention, the Swiss franc had surged more than 13% against the euro in 2011. After the SNB intervened, the Swiss franc immediately weakened, snapping four days of gains against the euro and causing the EUR/CHF to shoot up like a rocket, clearing over 1,000 pips in just three hours.

As shown in this report:

"The Swiss National Bank stunned financial markets by setting a ceiling for the Swiss franc against the euro in an attempt to prevent the strength of its currency from pushing its economy into recession. The central bank said it would set a minimum exchange rate of SFr1.20 against the euro."

Financial Times, September 6, 2011

Regulate Reserve Requirement Ratio

The reserve requirement ratio (RRR) is defined as the amount of liquid assets that a central bank mandates a bank to keep at all times. Expressed as a percentage of the bank's total deposits, the RRR ensures that the bank is able to pay an unusually high number of withdrawals should the need ever occur. It also helps to ensure that the bank does not overleverage itself. Increasing or decreasing the RRR has the effect of controlling the money supply, thereby regulating inflation.

Increasing the RRR

On May 11, 2011, China announced inflation figures of 5.4% for April 2011. This was higher than the median estimate of 5.2% that economists were expecting. A day later, China announced a 50 basis point hike in the RRR, raising it from 20.5% to 21%. Increasing the RRR essentially limits the supply of money in the financial system. This has the effect of cooling down inflationary pressures.

As shown in this report:

"The People's Bank of China just announced another hike in reserve requirement ratio by 50 basis points. Just as the data published yesterday invoked divided responses, ranging from rate cut to more tightening, the PBOC's announcement today confirms that they will continue with its tightening stance."

Business Insider, May 12, 2011

Decreasing the RRR

On February 18, 2012, China announced a 50 basis point reduction in the RRR, from 21% to 20.5%. The RRR reduction was estimated to free up about 350 to 400 billion yuan. The move was done to increase the supply of money in the financial system, spur lending, and crank up economic activity in the wake of slowing growth.

As shown in this report:

"China's central bank cut the amount of cash that commercial lenders must hold as reserves on Saturday for the second time in nearly three months. The PBOC delivered a 50-basis-point cut in banks' reserve requirement ratio (RRR), after repeatedly defying market expectations for such a move."

CNBC, February 18, 2012

COMMERCIAL AND INVESTMENT BANKS

Commercial banks are the biggest traders of forex currencies worldwide. Hooked up to the interbank market, these banks trade currencies with each other through electronic networks. The spreads, or the difference between the bid and ask prices, are razor-thin within the interbank market.

These narrow spreads allow banks to transact huge amounts of currencies at very low costs. The top-tier interbank market accounts for about 55% of all forex transactions worldwide. According to the 2012 Euromoney foreign exchange survey, Deutsche Bank retained its position as the world's largest forex trading bank for the eighth consecutive year.

Other players in the top 10 can be seen in Table 3.1.

There are basically two reasons why commercial banks participate in the forex market: to facilitate transactions for clients and to run a proprietary trading desk.

Facilitate Transactions for Clients

Banks offer a wide variety of forex services for their clients. These include, but are not limited to, spot transactions, forwards, options, and international money transfers. Their clients include small banks, corporations, financial institutions, and high-net-worth individuals.

These clients engage the currency market in order to hedge currency risk or to speculate on price movements for profit. A typical transaction between the bank and a client follows a simple three-step process:

1. **Contact.** This is the first initiation that a client makes with the bank. The call is usually done through a dedicated direct phone line or

TABLE 3.1　Top 10 Currency Traders: Percentage of Overall Volume, May 2012

Rank	Name	Market Share
1	Deutsche Bank	14.57%
2	Citi	12.26%
3	Barclays Investment Bank	10.95%
4	UBS AG	10.48%
5	HSBC	6.72%
6	JP Morgan	6.60%
7	Royal Bank of Scotland	5.86%
8	Credit Suisse	4.68%
9	Morgan Stanley	3.52%
10	Goldman Sachs	3.12%

Source: Euromoney FX Survey 2012

through an electronic dealing platform, such as Reuters Dealing 3000. The call could be to place an order or simply to request for market information and seek the salesperson's opinion on the direction of the market.

2. **Deal.** If there is a need to transact, the client will state the amount and the currency pair involved. The salesperson on hand then either quotes the client directly or calls over to the trading desk and obtains a live price. In general, clients who have an existing relationship with the bank or who transact larger volumes usually enjoy more competitive pricing than others.

3. **Execute.** When the client accepts the quoted price from the bank, the deal is executed.

By facilitating these transactions for clients, salespeople earn margin for the bank. The margin is the slack, or the amount in the client's quoted price that a salesperson can alter to benefit the bank.

Run a Proprietary Trading Desk

Banks run proprietary trading desks for only one reason: to generate profit. However, such speculative activities recently have come under fire because of the lack of risk management involved. Investment banks such as Goldman Sachs and Deutsche Bank are known to generate a large portion of their quarterly and annual profits through proprietary trading.

These proprietary trading desks are normally kept separate from customer flow. In 2008, the blowup of the global financial crisis uncovered the huge risks that banks undertook in their proprietary trading activities.

Bear Stearns, the fifth largest investment bank in the United States, was the first big casualty to go under. In March 2008, the Federal Reserve Bank of New York provided an emergency loan to the bank in a bid to avert a sudden collapse. However, the losses racked up from its issuance of asset-backed securities proved to be the death knell for the company.

In September 2008, Bear Stearns was sold to JP Morgan Chase for USD10 per share, a price far below its pre-crisis 52-week high of USD133.20 per share. The sale, which was higher than the original agreed upon price of USD2 per share, caused stock holders to lose about 90% of their investment.

Lehman Brothers, the fourth largest investment bank in the United States, was the next to follow when it went bankrupt on September 15, 2008. When it filed for Chapter 11, it had over 26,000 employees and USD639 billion in assets, making it the largest bankruptcy filing in the history of the United States.

On the same day, Merrill Lynch was sold to Bank of America in an all-stock deal worth USD50 billion. The other top three blowups from proprietary trading in recent years are listed next.

1. **Jerome Kerviel, Société Générale.** In 2008, Jerome Kerviel stunned the entire world by creating the largest loss for a major bank in financial history. In 2000, Kerviel joined the compliance department of Société Générale, the second largest bank in France. In 2005, he was promoted to the bank's Delta One trading team, which specialized in the futures markets.

    In the course of his trading career, Kerviel made unauthorized trades worth 30 billion euros, making 1.4 billion euros by the end of the year. Having cleverly disguised the size of his trade earnings with fake trades, he started 2008 with an even bigger and, of course, riskier appetite.

    With his computing skills and inside knowledge, Kerviel managed to hide 50 billion euros in unauthorized trades. On January 19, 2008, his employers uncovered his scheme and started winding down positions over three days beginning January 21.

    The losses associated with Kerviel's unauthorized trades amounted to 4.9 billion euros. With the exception of Bernie Madoff's Ponzi scheme, Kerviel's losses are considered to be the largest fraud in banking history.

    In May 2010, Kerviel published a book called *L'engrenage: Mémoires d'un Trader* (*Downward Spiral: Memoirs of a Trader*), in which he alleged that his superiors knew of his trading activities all along.

    In October 2012, the Paris appeals court ordered Kerviel to spend three years in prison and pay back a staggering 4.9 billion euros to his former employer, Sociéte Genéralé.

2. **Kweku Adoboli, UBS.** In September 2011, Swiss banking giant UBS announced that it had lost over USD2 billion as a result of the rogue trading activities by 31-year-old Kweku Adoboli. Adoboli joined UBS as a trainee in March 2006 and worked his way up to the bank's Delta One trading business, handling exchange-traded funds. When news of his unauthorized trading activities broke out, UBS's shares plummeted, wiping off over 3.3 billion euros from the bank's market value.

    On September 24, 2011, Oswald Gruebel, then the chief executive officer (CEO) of UBS, resigned to take responsibility for Adoboli's acts. It was later discovered that UBS had failed to act on a warning issued by its computer system about Adoboli's trading. On January 30, 2012, Adoboli pleaded not guilty to two counts each of fraud and false accounting. On November 20, 2012, he was found guilty after a 2-month trial. He was sentenced to 7 years in jail for fraud, and earned the tag of having caused the largest unauthorized trading loss in British history.

3. **Bruno Iksil, JP Morgan Chase & Co.** In May 2012, JP Morgan Chase & Co. CEO Jamie Dimon stunned the world when he announced to investors that bad trades made in London would result in losses of USD2 billion. The announcement caused the bank's share price to plummet 10% in a day, wiping off USD14 billion of its value. The person responsible for the huge loss was a French trader name Bruno Iksil, nicknamed "the London whale" or "Voldermort" after the character in the Harry Potter books.

Apparently, Iksil had taken bets so large on a credit derivatives index that the skew (the measure between where the index should be trading based on its underlying components and where it actually was trading) got too big for too long. At the time, hedge fund managers bet against Iksil, and his positions left him deep in the red when the economic outlook worsened dramatically. In June 2012, CNBC's Kate Kelly reported that JP Morgan Chase & Co. Chief Investment Office had sold off as much as 65% to 70% of its losing London whale position in the CDX IG-9 10-year index.

In July 2012, JP Morgan announced that the trading loss amounted to USD4.4 billion, more than twice the initial estimate. In the same month, Iksil and two other employees, Achilles Macris and Javier Martin-Artajo, were taken off the company's internal employment database.

After the true amount of the trading loss came to light, Dimon admitted he was "dead wrong" to dismiss concerns that were raised in April 2012 about the trades as a tempest in a teapot.

The Volcker Rule

Since 2008, the repeated unfolding of failed proprietary trading activities prompted American economist and former U.S. Federal Reserve chairman Paul Volcker to draw up what is now known as the Volcker Rule. In proposing the rule, Volcker stated that the speculative activities engaged by the banks, particularly derivatives, played a key role in the global financial crisis that lasted from 2008 to 2010.

Derivatives initially were designed to mitigate risk in the financial system, but their vast usage had produced exactly the opposite effect. Volcker also argued that Wall Street banks took on excessive risk and engaged in unfair business practices because regulators were unable to properly monitor the banks' complex instruments and activities.

Essentially, the Volcker Rule is a specific section of the Dodd-Frank Wall Street Reform and Consumer Protection Act, which restricts U.S.

banks from trading speculative investments that do not benefit their customers.

The rule states that banks are not allowed to simultaneously enter into an advisory and creditor role with clients, such as with private equity firms. The Volcker Rule aims to minimize conflicts of interest between banks and their clients by separating the various types of business practices financial institutions engage in. It also aims to protect individuals by creating a more transparent financial framework that can be regulated more easily.

On January 21, 2010, President Barack Obama publicly endorsed the Volcker Rule. A month later, on February 22, five former U.S. Treasury Secretaries—W. Michael Blumenthal, Nicholas Brady, Paul O'Neill, George Shultz, and John Snow—followed suit and endorsed the Volcker Rule by sending a letter to the *Wall Street Journal*.

The Volcker Rule is not without its critics. On April 10, 2012, Peter J. Wallison, a senior fellow at the American Enterprise Institute, sent a letter to the *Wall Street Journal* titled "The Volcker Rule Is Fatally Flawed." In the letter, Wallison argued for the repeal of the rule. Here's an excerpt from that letter:

> *"It's not as though proprietary trading of debt securities by banks is some new idea that sprang from the mind of a Wall Street quant. Bank regulators, including the Fed when it was headed by Mr. Volcker, have always permitted banks to buy and sell whole loans, bonds, notes and commercial paper, as well as securities backed by car loans, credit-card receivables and mortgages."*

Please refer to this link for the full article: http://online.wsj.com/article/SB10001424052702303815404577333321275373582.html

MULTINATIONAL CORPORATIONS

Multinational corporations (MNCs) participate in the forex market primarily for hedging purposes. Hedging is basically a type of activity that offsets the risk associated with currency movements. Hedging represents approximately 5% of all global forex transactions.

Some companies even have their own trading floors, with traders speculating in order to make profits and to reduce the risks related to exchange rate fluctuations. Daily movements in currencies can have a significant impact on their bottom line.

Examples 3.9 and 3.10 are some real-life examples.

EXAMPLE 3.9: SWISS WATCHMAKER SWATCH GROUP

In July 2011, Swatch CEO Nick Hayek reported that the strength of the Swiss franc could cost the company upwards of USD 1 billion.
As shown in this report:

> *Swatch Chief Executive Nick Hayek said: "I think 2011 will be a record year, but the franc is a real concern." He added: "If the situation stays like it is now, sales could be hit by as much as one billion Swiss francs, or $1.25 billion, due to the impact of the strong franc."*

> *Wall Street Journal,* July 28, 2011

EXAMPLE 3.10: JAPANESE CARMAKER NISSAN

Japan is an export-oriented country, and a strong yen can wipe billions of dollars off corporate balance sheets in the country. In February 2012, Nissan reported that for every 1 yen that strengthens against the U.S. dollar (e.g., if USD/JPY falls from 80 to 79), the company loses 20 billion yen in annual operating profit.
As shown in this report:

> *Chief executive Carlos Ghosn said "the yen's recent weakening trend doesn't go far enough. We need more [weakening] to reestablish the competitiveness of Japan. The dollar should be between ¥90 and ¥100," adding that he doesn't see the yen's recent weakening trend as just a short-term development.*

> *Wall Street Journal,* February 27, 2012

Next we look at how hedging is done on the futures market to offset currency risks.

Hedging Example for Exporters

Let's take an example of an export company in Germany (called A), which has sold a container of materials worth USD100,000 to an import company in the United States (called B). The deal is done on June 1, 2012, but the payment is settled only once the goods are delivered on September 1, 2012.

The risk to Company A is the fluctuation of the currency rate EUR/USD. If the euro strengthens against the U.S. dollar between June 1, 2012, and

September 1, 2012, Company A will receive fewer euros for the USD100,000 paid by Company B, thereby affecting Company A's bottom line.

If, however, the euro weakens against the U.S. dollar in the same period, Company A will receive more euros once the exchange rate is taken into account. There is no currency risk for Company B because it is based in the United States and the payment is made in U.S. dollars. Company B is assured that the amount to pay will always be USD100,000 regardless of when the payment is made.

To protect itself against such currency fluctuations, Company A can hedge this risk by going "long" on EUR/USD on the futures market. A long position is a bet that the EUR/USD currency pair will rise. This position is taken on the day the deal is done, which is June 1, 2012. On September 1, 2012, the day of the cash transaction between the two companies, two scenarios can happen.

Scenario 1: Euro Strengthens Against the U.S. Dollar Say the euro strengthens against the U.S. dollar between June 1, 2012, and September 1, 2012. With a stronger euro, Company A will receive fewer euros once the USD100,000 is converted to euros. However, it will net a profit on the futures market because of its long position.

The lesser cash received for the goods will be offset by the profit received on the futures market. This sum total will be almost equivalent to the sum paid by Company B had the transaction been done on June 1, 2012.

Scenario 2: Euro Weakens Against the U.S. Dollar In contrast, say the euro weakens against the U.S. dollar between June 1, 2012, and September 1, 2012. With a weaker euro, Company A will receive more cash once the USD100,000 is converted to euros. However, it will net a loss on the futures market because of its long position (which is essentially a bet that the euro will strengthen against the U.S. dollar).

The more cash received for the goods will offset the loss incurred on the futures market. This sum total will be almost equivalent to the sum paid by Company B had the transaction been done on June 1, 2012.

Let's take a look at the next sample transaction.

Futures exchange: Singapore Mercantile Exchange

1 lot = €25,000

1 pip = USD2.50

EUR/USD exchange rate on June 1, 2012 = 1.3000

Note: Had the transaction been done on June 1, 2012, the exporter would have received €76,923 (100,000/1.3000). Hence, the exporter needs to hedge an amount close to €76,923.

Since the contract size for 1 lot on Singapore Mercantile Exchange is €25,000, the exporter goes long on 3 lots for EUR/USD.

Figure 3.1 shows a hedging example for an exporter.

Because of the hedge, Company A gained certainty of price. If the transaction was done on June 1, 2012, the exporter would have received €76,923.

With a simple hedge done on the Singapore Mercantile Exchange, the EUR/USD could have strengthened or weakened 500 pips in three months, and the amount the exporter received would have been almost identical.

Let's have a look at the final summary.

- If goods had been transacted on June 1, 2012, the exporter would have received *€76,923.*

- On September 1, 2012, if EUR/USD had strengthened to 1.35, the exporter would have received *€76,852.*

- On September 1, 2012, if EUR/USD had weakened to 1.25, the exporter would have received *€77,000.*

The hedge executed by the exporter provided less than a €100 variance on either side of the amount of €76,923. This hedge is important to protect the company's bottom line from wild currency fluctuations.

If Company A did not enter into a hedge position on the futures market, it would have received either €74,074 (100,000/1.35) or €80,000 (100,000/1.25). It is this uncertainty that causes exporters to hedge on the currency market.

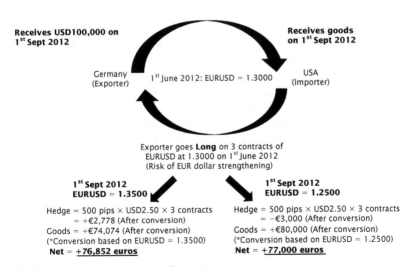

FIGURE 3.1 Hedging Example for an Exporter

In summary, for exporters, the affected revenue caused by currency fluctuations is canceled out by taking a long position in the futures market.

Hedging Example for Importers

Let's take an example of an import company in Germany (called A) that has bought a container of materials worth USD100,000 from an export company in the United States (called B). The deal is done on June 1, 2012, but the payment is only settled once the goods are delivered on September 1, 2012.

The risk to Company A is the fluctuation of the currency rate EUR/USD. If the euro weakens against the U.S. dollar between June 1, 2012, and September 1, 2012, Company A will have to pay more euros for the USD100,000 due to Company B, thereby affecting its bottom line.

If the euro strengthens against the U.S. dollar in the same period, Company A will pay fewer euros for the USD100,000 once the exchange rate is taken into account.

There is no currency risk for Company B because it is based in the United States and the incoming payment is made in U.S. dollars. It has the assurance that the amount it receives from Company A will always be USD100,000 regardless of when the payment is made.

To protect itself against currency fluctuations, Company A can hedge this risk by going short on EUR/USD on the futures market. A short position is a bet that the EUR/USD currency pair will drop.

This position is taken on the day the deal is done, which is June 1, 2012. On September 1, 2012, which is the day of the cash transaction between the two companies, two scenarios can happen.

Scenario 1: Euro Strengthens Against the U.S. Dollar Say the euro strengthens against the U.S. dollar between June 1, 2012, and September 1, 2012. With a stronger euro, Company A will pay fewer euros once the USD100,000 is converted to euros. However, it will incur a loss on the futures market because of its short position.

The lower payment for the goods will be countered by the loss incurred on the futures market. This sum total will be almost equivalent to the sum paid to Company B had the transaction been done on June 1, 2012.

Scenario 2: Euro Weakens Against the U.S. Dollar In contrast, say the euro weakens against the U.S. dollar between June 1, 2012, and September 1, 2012. With a weaker euro, Company A will pay more euros for the USD100,000 bill due to Company B. However, it will net a profit on the futures market because of its short position.

The more euros paid out is countered by the profit gained on the short position in the futures market. This sum total will be almost equivalent to the sum paid to Company B had the transaction been done on June 1, 2012.

Let's take a look at the next sample transaction.

Futures exchange: Singapore Mercantile Exchange

1 lot = $25,000

1 pip = USD2.50

EUR/USD exchange rate on June 1, 2012 = 1.3000

Note: Had the transaction been done on June 1, 2012, the importer would have paid €76,923 (100,000/1.3000). Hence, the importer needs to hedge an amount close to €76,923.

Since the contract size for one lot on Singapore Mercantile Exchange is €25,000, the importer goes short on 3 lots for EUR/USD.

Figure 3.2 shows a hedging example for an importer.

Because of the hedge, Company A gained certainty of price. If the transaction was done on June 1, 2012, the importer would have paid €76,923.

With a simple hedge done on the Singapore Mercantile Exchange, the EUR/USD could have strengthened or weakened 500 pips in three months and the amount the importer paid would have been almost identical.

FIGURE 3.2 Hedging Example for an Importer

- If goods had been transacted on June 1, 2012, the importer would have paid €76,923.
- On September 1, 2012, if EUR/USD had strengthened to 1.35, the importer would have paid €76,852.
- On September 1, 2012, if EUR/USD had weakened to 1.25, the importer would have paid €77,000.

The hedge executed by the importer provided less than a €100 variance on either side of the amount of €76,923. This hedge is important to protect the company's bottom line from wild currency fluctuations.

If Company A did not enter into a hedge position on the futures market, it would have paid either €74,074 (100,000/1.35) or €80,000 (100,000/1.25). It is this uncertainty that causes importers to hedge on the currency market.

In summary, for importers, the cost of goods caused by currency fluctuations is canceled out by taking a short position in the futures market.

INSTITUTIONAL TRADERS

Institutional investors in the forex market include investment and insurance companies, pension funds, endowment funds, mutual funds, and hedge funds. These institutions make up about 30% of all forex transactions worldwide.

As international players on the financial circuit, these institutions participate in the forex market for two reasons. The first reason is to trade for profit. The second reason is that with a global portfolio spanning several countries, fluctuations in the forex market require the investment managers to hedge their portfolios against currency risks.

An example of a modern-day hedge fund is FX Concepts, the world's largest currency hedge fund, which manages over USD12 billion in assets (as of 2012). In early 2011, chairman and chief investment officer John Taylor announced that its Global Currency Program earned 12.53% in 2010, topping the Barclay Hedge Fund Index by 2 percentage points.

A segment of the institutional crowd that has gained rapid popularity in recent years is called high-frequency trading (HFT). Sometimes referred to as algorithmic trading, HFT aims to earn small, short-term profits on a high number of trades.

Institutional-level HFT is rarely conducted over the public Internet, due to latency issues. It generally is outsourced to an institutional-grade data center. Due to the extreme necessity for speed in the execution of trades, most principals seek to co-locate their transaction servers at distances measured in yards of their liquidity provider's servers. Milliseconds can mean the difference between success and failure in HFT.

RETAIL FOREX BROKERS

Brokers allow individuals to access the forex market by passing clients' orders to commercial banks or institutional trading platforms, such as EBS, Reuters Dealing, and HotSpot. There are two basic models of brokers: straight-through processing (STP) or market making (MM). STP brokers pass the entire flow of their clients' orders straight through to the liquidity providers behind them. These brokers get paid from the spread or by charging a commission on each transaction. MM brokers operate differently. Besides earning a spread or commission on each transaction, MM brokers book clients' trades in house, which means that the brokers themselves become the counterparties to client trades.

On October 31, 2011, one of the world's largest derivatives brokers, MF Global, went under, becoming the seventh largest bankruptcy in U.S. history. Besides embracing a market-making model, what sealed MF Global's fate was a USD6.3 billion bet on the bonds of some of Europe's most indebted nations.

As shown in this report:

"MF Global filed for bankruptcy on Monday morning in New York, after the Federal Reserve Bank of New York as well as the major exchanges suspended dealings with the broker-dealer led by Jon Corzine. This followed its suspension as a primary dealer by the New York Fed, as well as the suspension on trading by MF Global on the Chicago Mercantile Exchange, ICE and NYSE Life, which said MF Global clients were limited to liquidation-only trading."

Financial Services, October 31, 2011

The market-making model of brokers carries huge risks. Profits can soar when trades go their way, but things can turn sour very quickly when trades go horribly wrong. The STP model, in contrast, is a steady business model with no downside risk. Unlike the market-making model, profits are not volatile because the broker itself does not act as the counterparty to the client's trades. Profits are made solely on the volume of trades executed by the clients.

Some of the world's largest retail forex brokers include FXCM, Oanda, Alpari, GFT, and FXPRIMUS.

RETAIL TRADERS

By all accounts, retail traders represent the fastest-growing segment of the entire forex market. One of the key factors for the explosive growth in recent years was the crash of 2008.

On September 29, 2008, the Dow Jones fell a jaw-dropping 778 points in a single day, closing at 10365. From October 2008 to March 2009, the Dow continued to shed 40% of its value. The global financial crisis caused decade-old institutions to go out of business, and many families saw their hard-earned wealth evaporate.

The financial crisis also triggered a massive wave of deleveraging that saw investors flock to the safety of the U.S. dollar, Japanese yen, and Swiss franc. As investors in other asset classes were reeling from the crisis, traders in the forex market remained largely unscathed. One of the key elements that kept the heads of forex traders above water was the ability to go long or short at any time.

This was, and continues to be, the very reason that draws thousands of people into the forex market daily. Today, retail forex traders account for about 8% of the total forex market—and still growing. According to a recent report by Forex Magnates on February 1, 2012, the retail forex market volume is USD217 billion daily and USD4,777 billion monthly.

SUMMARY

There are six main participants in the forex market: central banks, commercial banks and investment banks, multinational corporations, institutional traders, retail forex brokers, and retail traders.

Central banks take part in the forex market to stabilize their respective economies. They do this in three main ways: regulating interest rates, regulating reserve requirement ratios, and direct intervention by buying or selling currencies.

Commercial banks take part in the forex market for two reasons: to facilitate forex transactions for their clients and to speculate for profit. Banks speculate by running their own proprietary trading desks. However, inherent risks exist when they do this. Some of the biggest trading blowups in history occurred because bank traders were left unchecked when they took on too much risk by piling on one trading position after another.

Three of the most notable rogue traders in history are Jerome Kerviel of Société Générale, Kweku Adoboli of UBS, and Bruno Iksil of JPMorgan Chase & Co. Through their rouge trading activities, these three men racked up collective losses exceeding USD10 billion.

The repeated unfolding of such failed proprietary trading activities prompted American economist and former United States Federal Reserve chairman Paul Volcker to draw up the Volcker Rule, which is a specific section of the Dodd-Frank Wall Street Reform and Consumer Protection Act that restricts U.S. banks from trading speculative investments that do not benefit their customers.

Multinational corporations take part in the forex market primarily for hedging purposes. A hedge is basically a type of activity that offsets the risk associated with currency movements. Hedging is mostly done when companies receive money or pay for goods in currencies other than their own local currency.

Exporters take out long positions on their currency because the risk of a stronger currency erodes their net profit when payment is made in other currencies. Importers take out short positions on their currency because the risk of a weaker currency means they have to pay more for goods that are denominated in other currencies. With a simple hedge, corporations gain certainty of price. Doing this keeps their bottom line fairly predictable regardless of how the currency market moves.

Institutional traders, forex brokers, and retail traders all trade the forex market for the same reason: to generate profits. A segment of the institutional crowd that has gained rapid popularity in recent years is called high-frequency trading (HFT). Sometimes referred to as algorithmic trading, HFT aims to earn small, short-term profits on a high number of trades.

As a result of increasing demand from the retail crowd, transaction costs have decreased, technology offerings have improved, and value-added services on forex brokerage firms have increased tremendously over the years.

CHAPTER 4

Why You Must Play the Game

There are many reasons why retail traders are jumping on the forex bandwagon at an accelerated pace. This chapter lists the top 17 advantages. One of the biggest attractions lies in the market's unparalleled liquidity. The forex market is the largest market in the world and is open 24 hours a day, 5 days a week. Traders can also go short at any time and take advantage of the massive leverage available, sometimes as high as 500:1.

Brokers provide other advantages. Some of these advantages include free tools, quality resources, free practice accounts, and the beauty of starting live trading with a low capital outlay. This chapter also discusses the biggest advantage in trading the forex market: It gives you a firm grip on global finance and other asset classes because it deals with the lowest common denominator in every country: the currency.

TOP 17 REASONS TO TRADE FOREX

There are a myriad of reasons to explain why ordinary folks and fellow traders are jumping on board the forex market at an accelerated pace. Here we discuss 17 of these reasons.

1. Global 24-Hour Market

One of the biggest draws of the forex market is its 24-hour accessibility, Mondays to Fridays. This accessibility is possible because markets around the world open and close at different times to facilitate cross-border global trade. Trading starts in Sydney, Australia, on Monday morning, and as the day goes on, more financial markets open for business: Japan, Singapore, and other parts of Asia. The Middle East, Europe, and finally the Americas follow.

When the U.S. market starts to close, Australia begins again, and the process goes on 24 hours a day until the markets close at 5 p.m. New York time on Friday. Today, at any point of time, there is always a major financial center open where commercial banks, hedge funds, corporations, and retail traders engage in trading currencies.

The 24-hour availability means that traders can trade virtually any time of the day, without waiting for markets to open. This accessibility is particularly helpful to people who hold a day job. In contrast, the stock or futures market is opened for about eight hours a day only.

The next table shows the opening and closing times of the top three financial markets in the world: London, New York, and Tokyo.

Forex Market	Greenwich Mean Time
Tokyo open	23:00
Tokyo close	08:00
London open	07:00
London close	16:00
New York open	12:00
New York close	21:00

2. World's Most Liquid Market

The forex market today is undisputedly the largest financial market in the world. According to the 2010 Triennial Survey from the Bank for International Settlements, the official forex daily turnover was already USD4.0 trillion.

With such an immense amount of money in the financial system, there are always ready buyers and sellers to transact any amount at any price, especially the currencies of the major economies. Traders never have to worry about the inability to exit a trade once they enter.

Other asset classes, such as stocks, futures, options, and commodities, do not enjoy such massive liquidity. In fact, their illiquidity tends to restrict traders, especially during after hours.

The most liquid hours of the trading cycle occur when two major financial centers are open, such as during the period of Asia closing/Europe opening and Europe closing/U.S. opening.

3. Limited Slippage

"Slippage" is defined as the difference between the expected price of a trade and the price the trade actually executes at. However, due to the market's liquidity, slippage is almost a non-issue as most brokers honor instantaneous trade executions from real-time quotes that are displayed on the traders' screens. Slippage is inversely proportional to the volume available at each price level—the more volume there is, the less slippage a trader experiences.

During normal market conditions, there is usually no slippage. The only time slippage becomes an issue is when economic news is released. Such times lead to higher volatility than usual, and slippage may occur when markets move too fast.

When slippage does occur, a trader ends up paying more than the quoted spread. As an example, if the quoted spread for the EUR/USD is 2 pips and the trader gets slipped an additional 2 pips, the entire cost for the transaction becomes 4 pips.

4. Go Short Anytime

In the United States, the Securities and Exchange Commission (SEC) introduced a rule that disallowed selling short in the equity market, except on an uptick. This rule limits traders who are able to spot opportunities in the market when prices fall fast.

Such restrictions are not confined to the equity market. In the futures market, a limit-down/limit-up rule prevents prices from moving beyond a certain percentage from the previous day's settlement price. However, no such rules apply in the forex market. You can short a currency pair as much as you want at any time, without needing to wait for any upticks.

The main reason forex traders can go short at any time is because forex is traded in currency pairs. This means that in every currency transaction, there will always be one currency that gains over another.

As an example, when you go short on USD/CAD, you are in fact selling U.S. dollars and buying Canadian dollars. When you go long on USD/CAD, you are in fact buying U.S. dollars and selling Canadian dollars.

Depending on how the market moves, one currency will always be losing value over the other. It is for this reason that forex traders are able to go short at any time.

5. No Restrictions

The forex market is considered an over-the-counter (OTC) market, where trading is done via an interbank network. OTC trading is the opposite of exchange trading, which occurs on futures exchanges or stock exchanges.

When trading is done on an exchange, rules apply. Here's an example:

On August 12, 2011, four European countries—Italy, France, Spain, and Belgium—banned the short selling of stock in their markets to try to halt the precipitous plunge in value of troubled European banks. The move was similar to the decision made by the SEC when it banned the shorting of stocks in the United States during the 2008 financial crisis.

Such exchange-enforced rules do not apply to the forex market simply because, as an OTC market, forex is not traded on any exchange, and thus it is not governed by the rules of any exchange.

6. High Leverage

The forex market offers the highest leverage available for any financial instrument. Today, brokers offer leverage as high as 500:1. This means that traders can control $100,000 worth of currencies with only $200. Traders also have the flexibility to select the right amount of leverage to suit their style of trading.

Leverage is essential for retail traders to make good money from forex trading. This is because the average daily percentage move of a major currency is less than 1%, whereas a stock can easily have a 10% price move on any given day. With decent leverage, you do not need to fork out a huge amount to trade one standard lot.

Comparatively, high leverage is not available in the equity market. This means that equity traders have to fork out more margin to trade. Leverage is further reduced when the trader decides to short. Again, these restrictions do not exist in the forex market.

7. Low Cost

When you trade the forex market, the only transaction cost you pay is the spread. As discussed in Chapter 2, the spread is the difference between the buy price and the sell price, and it is the only fee charged by the broker for executing your trade.

In comparison, when equity traders execute a trade, both spread and commission are incurred as fees. Due to the intense competition from thousands of brokers worldwide, spreads have dropped dramatically in the last few years. That is good news for retail traders like you and me.

Today, most brokers offer a spread of only 2 to 3 pips on the EUR/USD, the most widely traded currency pair in the forex market.

Figure 4.1 shows a 2 pip spread for EUR/USD on FXPRIMUS.

FIGURE 4.1   EUR/USD Spread on FXPRIMUS Market Watch

8. Absolute Convenience

As an OTC market, the forex market has no physical location; all trading is done electronically. All you need is an Internet connection and your favorite device and you can execute a trade anywhere in the world.

With the explosion of technology, almost everyone is connected to the Internet, and brokers have made it easy to access their platform via laptops, mobile phones, iPhones, iPads, and BlackBerrys.

I know many forex traders who travel the world while staying connected to their business of making money online. This freedom is truly something which the forex market can offer to anyone.

9. Practice Accounts

Every good broker offers a free practice or demo account. The practice account means two things: You trade with virtual money but you see live prices. Practice accounts allow new traders to get a taste of the forex market before jumping in with real funds.

Practice accounts are useful because they help both new and advanced traders alike. For new traders, practice accounts help them to build confidence and familiarity. For advanced traders, practice accounts help them to refine or test new strategies before using those exact systems to trade live.

Figure 4.2 shows a $50,000 demo account on FXPRIMUS.

FIGURE 4.2 $50,000 Demo Account on FXPRIMUS

10. Market Transparency

Whenever governments, central bank chiefs, or finance ministers make economic/monetary policies that affect currencies, the announcements are readily available on almost every media imaginable within a few minutes. The bonus is that in most cases, warning signals or hints about future actions are dropped in advance. Here's an example:

On August 4, 2011, the Bank of Japan (BOJ) sold 4.5 trillion yen to weaken its currency. This caused the USD/JPY to shoot up 300 pips in one day.

On October 31, 2011, Japan intervened again, selling a record 8 trillion yen. This move caused the yen to plunge more than 4% and caused the USD/JPY to shoot up over 350 pips in just three hours.

The fact of the matter is this: Prior to the interventions, BOJ governor Masaaki Shirakawa and the two finance ministers who were in charge at the time—Yoshihiko Noda on August 4 and Jun Azumi on October 31, 2011—had been preparing the markets for the move weeks before they acted.

They had dropped strong hints of an upcoming intervention to combat one-sided speculative trades on the Japanese yen. The reason why they were so transparent with their intentions was to signal the traders to stand on the same side as them and collectively go long on USD/JPY.

When traders participate in a coordinated action, chances of a sustainable rally become higher, and the central bank does not have to spend as much money to weaken the yen.

Market transparency in stocks or commodities, however, is a lot lower. For example, no large institution will signal its intention to acquire a stock at a certain price. If word gets out and traders take part in a similar coordinated action and start bidding up the stock price, the stock would become more expensive for the institution to acquire.

As shown in this report:

> *"Finance Minister Yoshihiko Noda said that the yen is "strongly overvalued" and made it clear he has been in touch with overseas authorities on currency matters, fueling speculation the government may act to stem the yen's steady rise."*

> *Wall Street Journal*, August 2, 2011

11. No One Can Corner the Market

Due to its sheer size, no single entity, not even a central bank, can control the market price for an extended period. Take a look at Figure 4.3, which shows the intervention by the BoJ on August 4, 2011. Within four days, the price of USD/JPY had floated back down to the pre-intervention price.

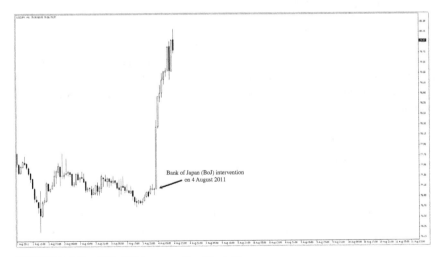

FIGURE 4.3 USD/JPY Intervention Took Place

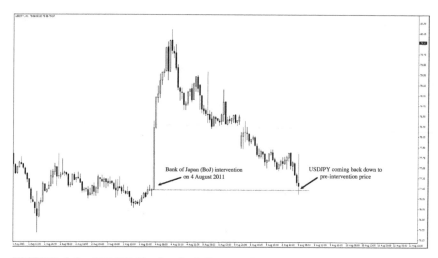

FIGURE 4.4 USD/JPY Coming Back Down to Pre-Intervention Price
Source: Created with FX Primus Ltd, a PRIME Mantle Corporation PLC company. All rights reserved.

This is one of the main reasons why central banks are becoming less and less inclined to intervene and manipulate market prices.

Figure 4.4 shows a chart on USD/JPY coming back down to pre-intervention price in just five days.

12. Tools and Resources

Most forex brokers today provide a plethora of resources for traders to access. These include breaking news, trade alerts, live webinars, videos, and tutorials just to name a few. Traders today have a wide range of resources to get them up to speed to trade profitably.

In my experience, to be consistently profitable in the forex market, you need:

1. The ability to decode breaking news
2. The skill to execute live trades
3. The mentorship of a coach

Some brokers offer resources that fulfill part or all three of these requirements. This is great news for new and experienced traders alike because getting a world-class education enables you to achieve consistent profits in the forex market.

Additionally, some brokers offer the ability to trade several asset classes all on the same platform. As you mature as a trader, it is only natural that you become more aware of capital flows and how they move into gold, oil, and commodities. You will appreciate the convenience of monitoring several markets all on one platform provided by the broker.

13. No Middlemen

You don't have to pick up a phone to tell someone on the other end to execute or close a trade for you. Although you are trading through your broker's platform, you are in total control of the transaction the entire time.

You decide when you would like to go long on the GBP/USD or short on the NZD/USD. You have full control and autonomy over your account, which puts you in the driver's seat to achieve consistent profits in the forex market.

14. Low Start-up Cost

One of the biggest advantages of getting started in forex trading is the low barrier to entry. Ten years ago, it was rare for someone to open a forex trading account for under USD100,000. However, with the explosion of forex brokers all over the world, you no longer have to lay out a lot of cash when you start trading live. Today, some brokers offer you the opportunity to open a real account with as little as USD100. Additionally, you won't incur any setup fees, monthly payments, or software rental fees.

The brokers provide the trading software for free, and it comes with the practice account that we discussed earlier. Most forex brokers worldwide use the Meta Trader 4 platform, which is the most popular trading software loved by traders all around the world.

15. Global Finance Decoded

I speak from personal experience when I say that I could never really understand global finance until the day I started trading forex. As a trader, understanding market sentiment is key and knowing when risk is on or off helps me tremendously in my trading decisions.

Let's take a look at an example. When you trade forex, you will be privy to the interest rates attached to each currency. Generally the currencies with higher interest rates are categorized as the risk currencies while those with lower interest rates are termed the safe haven currencies.

When risk appetite is strong in the markets, currencies with low interest rates—the low yielders—will be sold off in preference for the risk currencies, which give a better return. This trade is commonly known as the carry trade.

Conversely, when risk is off, the opposite effect happens. Risk currencies are sold off, and money moves back to the low yielders. The distinction is subtle but important: Currencies with high interest rates do not climb all the time.

In times of fear and panic, risk is off and traders are more concerned with parking their money in a safe place as opposed to earning a higher return. Trading the forex market helps you to decode such sentiment.

16. Recession-Proof Income

One of my earliest mentors told me an important money lesson that I'll never forget: "Mario, if you want to be rich, you've got to get yourself on a platform that is recession-proof." Knowing what I know now, I believe that trading the forex market is the best recession-proof platform to generate consistent income.

Why is this true? There is always an opportunity to go long or short. There is always an opportunity to make money. Forex traders are never affected by recessions, market cycles, or downturns.

17. All for One, and One Forex

This last point is the most important. It also takes slightly longer to explain. Trading the forex market gives you insights into other financial markets, such as stocks, oil, gold, commodities, and fixed income securities like bonds.

When you trade currencies, you are trading a unit of a country. This gives you the ability to see global capital flows.

Stocks   Here's an example of how forex helps in trading the stock market. Let's take an example of a trader who is based in Singapore but decides to buy shares in global giant Apple, which is based in the United States.

To do this, the trader needs to exchange Singapore dollars (SGD) to U.S. dollars before using U.S. dollars to buy the Apple stock. In this regard, the trader is already exposed to the forex market through the USD/SGD exchange rate.

Fast forward three months. Our trader makes a 20% gain from the Apple stock. To realize the profit, the trader sells off the shares and converts the

U.S. dollars back into Singapore dollars. However, during the three months, the Singapore dollar actually strengthened against the U.S. dollar.

Although our trader made 20% gains from Apple stock, the stronger Singapore dollar would have eroded a portion of his cash. Knowledge of the forex market could have induced the trader to take a short position on the USD/SGD currency pair so that he would not be susceptible to the wild swings of the USD/SGD exchange rate.

Commodities   Three factors affect the price of commodities worldwide:

1. Demand and supply
2. Value of the U.S. dollar
3. Speculation on the futures market

The U.S. dollar is used in vast amounts in international trade, and almost all global commodities are priced in U.S. dollars. Hence, understanding its role in the commodities arena is key. In general, the price of commodities is inversely proportional to the value of the U.S. dollar. This means that when the value of the U.S. dollar goes down, the price of commodities tend to rise.

There are two reasons for this. First, a weak dollar makes U.S. exports cheaper for foreign countries, which boosts sales of commodities, such as corn, wheat, and soybeans, and causes their prices to rise.

Understanding the nature of the U.S. dollar as a safe haven and a reserve currency helps us with the second reason—when risk is on, fund managers move money out of safe haven assets and into risk assets. This causes the U.S. dollar to be sold off (causing it to fall in value) in favor of risk assets, such as commodities. When speculation on commodities is rife in the futures market, price tends to rise.

We discuss strategies for other commodities in Chapter 8.

Bonds   The key driver of bond prices is the prevailing interest rate in the country. Trading the forex market helps keep us abreast of the interest rate environment because it's one of the drivers of currency flows.

It also helps us to be ahead of the curve. Here's an example:

In Chapter 2, we discussed how high inflation normally brings about expectations for higher interest rates. Forex traders are among the first to take advantage of any impending rate hikes because rate hikes tend to strengthen the currency, and forex traders do not want to miss out on the chance to go long.

Once interest rates are hiked, the natural path is for bond prices to drop. Armed with this information ahead of time, forex traders can make calculated decisions on the benefits of owning a cheaper bond when prices drop. This is how forex trading helps with the buying and selling of bonds.

SUMMARY

With a daily trading volume in excess of USD4 trillion, the forex market offers unparalleled advantages. Due to the sheer size of the forex market, its immense liquidity offers three advantages:

1. Buyers and sellers are able to execute any order size at any price.
2. Slippage is drastically reduced.
3. Hardly any insider trading occurs. The same cannot be said with other asset classes, such as equities or commodities.

Another important aspect of the forex market is that it is the only financial market in the world that is open 24 hours a day, five days a week. International trade takes place continuously between countries, and the ability to buy and sell currencies must be available.

As quotes are given in currency pairs, traders have the ability to go long or short at any time, with absolutely no restrictions on going short. Considered an OTC market, the forex market also enjoys the privilege of not falling under the jurisdiction of any financial exchange.

When instruments are traded on an exchange, rules and regulations of both the country and the exchange apply. This sometimes can be more of a hindrance than a help to retail traders.

High leverage is also another advantage when trading the forex market. Leverage is provided by brokers. The higher the leverage employed, the less margin needed to control one standard lot of currencies.

To date, the leverage available on the forex market far outweighs the leverage available on either the equities or the futures market. Other benefits that brokers provide include low transaction costs, low account start-ups, free practice accounts, and free tools and resources. As the retail forex brokerage space becomes more and more competitive, brokers start to compete with one another to offer the best products and services to retail traders.

All this is good news for traders, who now have a wide array of choices to consider when starting on a forex journey.

Today, the forex market continues to attract retail traders all over the world at an unprecedented pace for three reasons:

1. The ability to go long and short anytime means that the forex market is practically a recession-proof vehicle.

2. Traders can access the forex market with just an Internet connection and an electronic device (e.g., laptop, tablet, or mobile phone).

3. Most important, forex trading gives traders an in-depth understanding of other asset classes, such as equities, bonds, and commodities because currencies are truly the lowest common denominator in any country. An understanding of forex gives traders a huge advantage in decoding global finance and capital flows.

CHAPTER 5

Play It Your Way

Understanding Your Profile

This chapter provides insight into the five different categories of forex traders: scalpers, day traders, swing traders, position traders, and mechanical traders. After reading it, you will understand the differences among the five and the three advantages of each category. This chapter also includes a test to help you determine which category you belong to. Once you discover your category, you will learn how your personality can help or affect your trading.

I have had the privilege to speak to large audiences all over the world. The most common question thrown at me is "Should I buy now or sell now?" Each time I hear the question, I can't help but smile. After all, that was my biggest question when I first started trading forex. "Tell me what to do now, and we'll talk about trading later!"

My answer, as always, goes like this: "You can buy now if your trading strategy tells you to buy now. You can also sell now if your trading strategy tells you to do so."

This answer always draws one of two responses: confused looks or exasperated ones.

However, the answer is precisely that—you can buy or sell at anytime. Let's see why.

As shown in Figure 5.1, Trader A goes long at Point X and exits at Point Y. Simultaneously, Trader B goes short at Point X but exits at Point Z. In both cases, each trader ended up with a profit.

In each case, both traders entered at exactly the same time and price. The only reason why both traders ended up making a profit is because they had different exit prices. This example also tells us that both traders executed their trades using different strategies.

You see, one of the key elements of successful trading is having a specific strategy that tells you what to do. Human beings are emotional

FIGURE 5.1   Traders Making Profit at Different Exit Prices

creatures. This is the reason why fear, greed, and hope are antithetical to successful trading.

When you follow a concise strategy, nothing is left to emotional triggers and everything boils down to following the rules of the strategy. The sentence "When you fail to plan, you plan to fail" rings true in the trading world as well as in life.

However, over the years as a trader and coach, I unearthed a disturbing pattern that seemed to permeate the global trading community: Even with a successful trading strategy, traders still seemed to suffer consistent losses rather than consistent profits.

THE EXPERIMENT

This finding led me to conduct an experiment at my forex academy. The experiment involved two traders whom I shall call Mike and Amanda. The test was simple. All Mike and Amanda had to do was to follow the trading plan I gave them. The trading plan consisted of a trading strategy, complete with specific rules on how to enter for a long trade and how to enter for a short trade.

We even spent two days together to ensure that they fully understood the rules of the trading plan. In fact, to ensure that I left no stone unturned,

I sent both traders alerts via their mobile phones to watch for any upcoming trade setup.

At the end of one month, their results were very different. Mike ended up having a net return of 10% for his account; Amanda managed a return of only 2%. This result was all the more interesting considering that both Mike and Amanda:

1. Started with the same capital

2. Took exactly the same number of trades

3. Entered all the trades correctly

4. Faithfully called me after they entered every trade

How could this be?

After an in-depth study on their trades, I found that the biggest reason for the difference in their accounts was that Amanda constantly meddled with her trades. Although she executed the entries perfectly, she messed up the exits. A common and truthful statement she shared with me was "I was too impatient to wait for the trade to exit so I got out earlier."

Mike, however, had no problems following through on trades after he entered them. Essentially, he did not meddle with his trades after he entered them but allowed them to hit either their stops or their targets.

In short, although both traders had the same strategy, Amanda's personality caused her to exit some trades prematurely. Those actions caused her account to have a different result from Mike's, although both had access to the same resources and the same trading strategy.

The result of that experiment became the driving force to write this book. The message is simple: Having a successful strategy is only the first step. Pairing a successful strategy with your personality is far more important.

In essence, there is no perfect strategy. The perfect strategy is the one that perfectly suits you.

Sports Illustrated

Let's look at an example in sports. If I were a sports coach and a budding athlete came up to me and asked, "Hey, coach, which sport should I play so that I can achieve mega success in the sporting world?"

As a coach, I would consider five options. Option 1 could be baseball.

One of its greats, Babe Ruth, has been named the greatest baseball player of all time in various surveys and rankings. In 1998, the *Sporting News* ranked him number one on the list of "Baseball's 100 Greatest

Players." In 1969, he was named baseball's Greatest Player Ever in a ballot commemorating the hundredth anniversary of professional baseball. In 1993, the Associated Press reported that Muhammad Ali was tied with Babe Ruth as the most recognized athlete in America.

In his career, Ruth had an eye-popping batting average of 0.342 en route to winning the World Series seven times.

Option 2 could be soccer. One of its greats, Lionel Messi, has numerous accolades. In 2010, *France Football* ranked him at the top of its list of the world's richest soccer players, ahead of David Beckham and Cristiano Ronaldo, with $29.6 million in combined income from salaries, bonuses, and off-field earnings.

In 2011, Messi won the prestigious Fifa Ballon d'Or, making him the first player in the world to win three straight Fifa world player trophies. In 2012, Messi made Union of European Football Associations (UEFA) Champions League history by becoming the first player to score five goals in one match.

The third option could be motor racing. The official Formula 1 website states that Michael Schumacher is "statistically the greatest driver the sport has ever seen." He holds many of the sport's records, including race victories, fastest laps, pole positions, points scored, and most races won in a single season—13 in 2004.

In 2002, he became the only driver in Formula 1 history to finish in the top three in every race of a season and then also broke the record for most consecutive podium finishes. To date, he is the sport's only 7-time world champion.

Option 4 could be track and field. Usain Bolt is a Jamaican sprinter who has netted five gold medals in two World Championships and six gold medals in two Olympics. At the time of this writing, he is the world record and Olympic record holder in the 100 meters, the 200 meters, and (along with his teammates) the 4×100 meter relay. He is also the reigning Olympic champion in these three events.

In 2009, Bolt stunned the world in Berlin with a record-breaking effort in the 100 meter final, finishing in an astonishing 9.58 seconds.

The fifth and final option could be boxing. Manny Pacquiao is boxing's first 8-division world champion, having won six world titles. He is also the first fighter to win the lineal championship in four different weight classes. He was named "Fighter of the Decade" for the 2000s by the Boxing Writers Association of America (BWAA). He is also a 3-time "The Ring" and BWAA "Fighter of the Year," winning the award in 2006, 2008 and 2009. Today, Pacquiao is rated as the best pound-for-pound boxer in the world.

In all five of these examples, the athletes would be considered extremely successful in their chosen sporting field. Some even feature regularly in the annual *Forbes* list of the world's highest-paid athletes, earning millions of dollars from salaries, bonuses, and sponsorships. However, pointing young athletes a certain way just because others have been successful in that field may not yield similar results.

In fact, it would be hard to even imagine soccer great Lionel Messi having the same level of boxing success as Manny Pacquiao, should he decide on a career switch one day.

Recently, global TV giant Entertainment and Sports Programming Network (ESPN) came up with a list of ten skills that it determined make up a successful sports person. These were:

1. Endurance
2. Strength
3. Power
4. Speed
5. Agility
6. Flexibility
7. Hand–eye coordination
8. Nerve (defined as the ability to maintain composure in a fearful environment)
9. Durability (defined as the ability to withstand constant physical punishment)
10. Analytic aptitude (defined as the ability to evaluate and react to strategic situations)

ESPN then analyzed 60 sports and asked a group of experts made up of sports scientists, kinesiology academics, and sporting journalists to assign a number from 1 to 10 to each of these skills.

The Results Among the 60 sports analyzed, baseball came out tops in the hand–eye coordination category with a rating of 9.25. Soccer led the pack in the agility category with a rating of 8.25. Motor racing was number 1 in the nerve category with a rating of 9.88. Track and field sprinting was placed first in the speed category, also with a rating of 9.88. Finally, boxing emerged victorious in the durability category with a rating of 8.5.

Hence, to ensure the highest chance of success in any given sport, a sports coach would put an athlete through a series of tests to determine his or her strengths and weaknesses. If the athlete scored the highest in the hand–eye coordination category, the baseball route would be apt. If the athlete came out tops in the agility category, soccer would be the top choice. If the athlete had the best score in the nerve category, a career in motor racing might beckon.

Track and field sprinting would be the answer had the athlete aced the speed category, and, finally, an illustrious boxing career wouldn't be too far off if the athlete led in the durability category. Your best chance of achieving greatness in the sporting world is choosing the sport that best resonates with your dominant strengths.

Forex trading is like sports. There are many fields where success can be achieved in the forex market. A certain strategy in the forex world corresponds to a certain discipline in the sporting world, whether it is soccer or boxing. Similarly, the best chance of succeeding in forex trading is selecting a toolbox of strategies that complements your personality.

FIVE CATEGORIES OF FOREX TRADERS

Style is important. We hear about style on a daily basis from the mass media. Not a day goes by without the newspapers, magazines, radio, or TV promoting a perfume, apparel, a luxury car, a watch, or a mobile phone. Advertisers know that style is an integral part of our personality.

This is why products are painstakingly created with different textures, smells, or purposes. Everyone is different, and the best product is the one that best suits your needs. The products that you buy tell a lot about the kind of style that you like and reveal much about your personality. They define who you are.

It is the same with forex trading: No two traders have exactly the same style. That's why it's important for you to choose a style of trading that resonates with your personality and defines who you are. Forex traders the world over fall into one of five categories: scalpers, day traders, swing traders, position traders, and mechanical traders. The main difference between the categories of traders is the time frame employed while trading.

Essentially, the length of time in which a trading position is held increases from a scalper to a day trader, to a swing trader, and finally to a position trader. Mechanical traders are oblivious to the passing of time. Their trades are based on a fixed routine, regardless of time frame and regardless of market activity.

Scalpers

Scalpers are traders who like fast action. They enter and exit the forex market multiple times a day, taking a few pips each time. Typically, profits can range anywhere from a single pip to 10 pips. These trades can last anywhere from several seconds to several minutes. In terms of time frames, scalpers prefer looking at M1 and M5 charts (minute charts and 5-minute charts).

Their actions are mostly centered around the overlapping sessions of the major regions, typically during the Asia close/Europe open, Europe close/U.S. open. Scalpers trade during these hours mainly because these are the busiest hours in the forex market on any given day. This business tends to generate more volume, which in turn presents more trading opportunities.

As they need to react to market movements quickly, scalping is most suitable for traders who can devote their undivided attention and focus on the charts for a couple of hours at a time. In addition, scalpers need the ability to think on their feet and switch the direction of their trades fast if the situation calls for it.

Due to the numerous times in which scalpers enter and exit the markets, there are three simple rules in their toolbox:

1. **Spreads.** The spread on currency pairs is a significant factor in the scalper's strategy. Scalpers tend to stay away from currency pairs with large spreads and focus only on the major pairs, such as EUR/USD, GBP/USD, and USD/JPY. They do this because the spread on the majors is normally the tightest, and the majors have the highest liquidity.

2. **News.** Scalpers tend to avoid trading during major news announcements. This is because major news can evoke different emotions in the markets and cause wild swings in currency pairs. The unwelcome volatility during such news announcements can be the difference between a winning trade and a losing one.

3. **Leverage.** Scalpers tend to use high leverage because they are in and out of the market repeatedly with only a small profit. The high leverage amplifies their returns significantly.

Due to the fast-paced nature of scalping, it is not uncommon for traders to employ automated trading systems to execute trades on their behalf.

Scalping offers these top three advantages:

1. **Risk exposure.** Due to the nature of scalping, traders stay in the market for brief periods each time. This reduces their risk of getting stopped out by any unforeseen adverse events.

2. **Easier bites.** Markets can't make big moves without first making small ones. As commonsensical as that sounds, it is also why scalpers love small moves—they happen more frequently, so scalpers' chances of winning are bumped up.

3. **Frequency.** For markets to achieve significant up or down moves, a major change in expectations is required. Such changes normally are caused by primers, such as a major news release. The good news for scalpers is that even in the absence of news, profits can still be made.

Day Traders

The main distinguishing characteristic of day traders is that they don't like to hold a trading position overnight. Day traders typically put on a trade at the start of the trading day and tend to close it out before the day is over. To day traders, finishing the day without an open position is more important than the actual result of the trade itself. This means that the trade could either be a profit or a loss.

Depending on the currency pair, the profit potential per trade for day traders can range from 20 pips to 40 pips or more. In terms of time frames, day traders prefer looking at the M15 and the M30 charts (the 15-minute and the 30-minute chart respectively).

Unlike scalpers who avoid the news, day traders love trading the news. Keeping abreast of the daily news releases actually help them to plan their trades more effectively. Additionally, many day traders depend on news announcements as triggers for their trades.

Day traders are big momentum traders. This means that they look for a certain directional bias and go long or short based on the current movement, or wave, at that time. Part of the strategy entails looking for possible breakouts from tight ranges, especially when certain news announcements fare better or worse than forecasted numbers.

Day trading offers these top three advantages:

1. **Peace of mind.** Day traders sleep soundly at night knowing that they do not have any open market positions. As long as a position remains open in the forex market, it is exposed to risk. Examples of risk include market gapping, which happens when prices are non-existent during brief periods because of market volatility.

   If a trader's stop loss is located in the gap, the trade might not close out. If this happens, the trader has a higher risk exposure. Since day traders close out their positions by the end of the trading day, market gapping risk is hardly present.

2. **Easy analysis.** Day traders love the news, because news often injects momentum and causes currencies to move up or down. As positions are closed out every day, day traders do not subject themselves to analysis paralysis. This trading disease happens to many news traders

who grapple with the concept of how much markets tend to price in upcoming news or released news.

Since day traders are momentum traders who take advantage of the first moves, analysis is easy and straightforward.

3. **Structured calculations.** This is also one of the benefits of starting with a clean slate every day. When trades are left hanging in the market, equity and margin levels constantly fluctuate to reflect the current size of the open position. This fluctuation can confuse traders who need to make adjustments when they calculate their lot size for the next trade.

Day traders do not have this problem because trades are closed out at the end of the day, and lot sizes are calculated on a clean slate the next day.

Swing Traders

Swing traders normally hold trades beyond a day but never beyond a week. This trading style is most suited to part-time traders who have full-time jobs because not much time is needed to analyze the markets and set up the trade.

Depending on the currency pair, the profit potential per trade for swing traders can range from 50 pips to 150 pips or more. In terms of time frames, swing traders prefer looking at the H1 and the H4 charts (the hourly and the 4-hourly charts respectively).

Swing traders tend to be a bit more conservative than scalpers or day traders; they typically wait for several confirmation signals before triggering a trade.

At the same time, swing traders are not bothered by intraday volatility and price swings because they are more concerned with catching the medium-term trends. Profit targets and stop-loss levels are naturally larger for swing traders because they have a slightly longer-term view than day traders.

Since trades usually have larger targets, spreads won't have as much of an impact to overall profits for swing traders. As a result, trading pairs with larger spreads and lower liquidity is acceptable.

Swing trading offers these top three advantages:

1. **Favorable risk to reward.** Swing traders normally are not concerned with intraday movements of the market because they have a slightly longer time horizon in watching the markets.

As their time horizon is longer than that of day traders, swing traders normally set favorable risk to reward ratios of 1:2, 1:3, or more.

If the stop loss is set at 50 pips, the profit target is normally 100 pips, 150 pips, or more.

2. **Save time.** Swing traders are mostly technical traders, which means they do not have to spend time every day to keep abreast of financial news.

This is not to say that news is not important, but due to the swing trader's trading style of exiting positions in two to five days, daily news events don't matter much. This is one of the biggest draws of swing trading and makes the method perfect for new traders or part-time traders who have full-time jobs.

3. **Hassle-free.** Many traders feel the need to meddle with ongoing trades or to trigger unnecessary ones. This normally happens when traders trade several times a day.

As swing traders depend on a trading plan to trigger long and short positions, they do not fall into this trap. In fact, swing traders thrive on following a structured plan. Following a plan keeps human error to a minimum and enables swing traders to avoid emotional trading.

Position Traders

Position traders have the longest time horizon of the different categories. The total opposite of scalpers, position traders can sit on a trade for several weeks to several months. They have a very strong grasp of market fundamentals and are able to spot changes that could lead to highly profitable long-term gains once trades are locked in. Depending on the currency pair, the profit potential per trade for position traders can range from 500 pips to several thousand pips or more.

In terms of time frames, position traders prefer looking at the D1, W1, and even the MN charts (daily, weekly, and monthly charts respectively). Position traders are usually sophisticated investors with two distinct characteristics: Their astute reading of the financial markets makes them totally unconcerned with the short-term or even the medium-term movements of the currency market, and they own a large trading account. This size is necessary because capital is needed to withstand large floating losses should trades go against the trader for an extended period of time.

Position trading offers these top three advantages:

1. **Lower transaction costs.** Brokers charge a spread for every position executed in the forex market. Thus, scalpers incur the highest costs by virtue of their trading frequency. Position traders are on the opposite

end of the pole. Instead of executing many trades, position traders execute very few trades and prefer to manage those trades effectively. They do this by tightening the stop loss for open positions, which is a technique of dynamically shifting the stop loss level to chase the price.

As an example, for long positions, the stop loss is continuously shifted upwards. For short positions, the stop loss is continuously shifted downwards. This technique helps position traders to lock in profits along the way.

2. **Earn swap.** In every forex transaction, the trade involves borrowing one currency to buy another. Interest or swap is paid on the currency that is borrowed and earned on the one that is bought.

   As an example, if you are buying a currency with a higher interest rate than the one you are borrowing, the net interest rate differential will be positive, and you earn interest for every day that the trade remains open. This is sometimes called the carry trade. Position traders stand to gain a huge amount of swap when they hold trades for an extended period of time.

3. **Character building.** Emotions sometimes set in when trades are held for a long time. Both greed and fear can take over during the course of the trade. Position traders have to learn to manage greed when a sizable profit builds up. They have to weigh the decision of exiting the trade early to bank the profits against holding the trade longer for even bigger returns.

   The opposite is also true. When trades go against position traders, fear is bound to set in. They then have to weigh the decision of exiting the trade early to realize the loss against holding on to the position in the event markets reverse. Over their trading journeys, position traders must cultivate patience.

Mechanical Traders

Mechanical traders are usually beginners in the forex market. Their main focus in trading the markets is not time driven but system driven.

After mechanical traders go through a period of back-testing with historical data, they deem a particular strategy sound. Thereafter, these traders focus only on the execution of that strategy based on its rules. This method allows them to enter and exit trades without emotions or stress.

Due to the robotic application of mechanical trading, it is not uncommon to find mechanical traders coding their strategies into automated trading systems that can be fired off on cue. Once these systems are trading automatically, traders have the added advantage of further back-testing the automated systems with more historical data to ensure that it remains robust.

However, the very nature of robotic application is a double-edged sword. Since no discretionary trading takes place, an automated system can lull mechanical traders into a false sense of security.

This false security becomes a problem when market conditions change, as when interest rates are raised or lowered or when central banks inter-vene to pump liquidity into the financial system. Such acts undoubtedly affect the currency volatility and trading ranges.

If automated systems are not tweaked periodically to reflect chang-ing market conditions, mechanical traders can be in for a rough time with prolonged losses on their trading account.

Mechanical trading offers these top three advantages:

1. **No monitoring needed.** Once mechanical traders are confident that the system works, absolutely no monitoring of the market is needed, because mechanical traders are mostly system driven. Trades are executed faithfully (sometimes several times a day) regardless of how the market moves.

2. **Flexible trading.** Since mechanical traders are not dependent on any specific time frame, they are able to formulate trading systems to exploit the movements of any currency pair. This gives them the flex-ibility to trawl all available currency pairs on the broker's platform and build a mechanical system around it.

3. **Free time.** A fair amount of mechanical traders utilize expert advisors (EAs) on their trading platform to assist in trade execution. EAs are essentially automated trading systems. Because the model is hands-free, these mechanical traders have the time to pursue other work interests and hobbies.

YOUR PERFECT STRATEGY

We are how we trade and we trade how we are. No two traders are exactly alike. Your unique personality will cause you to trade differently from someone else. If you enjoy a fast-paced life filled with action from the word Go!, you most likely fall into the scalper category.

If you are holding down a job and don't have too much time to monitor the markets, you most likely fall into the swing trader category. It is import-ant to note that no one category is better or worse than the other. They are all the same in terms of making you a consistently profitable trader.

The key here is to discover which category you are in, based on your lifestyle and personality, so that you can flow with your dominant strength when trading the forex market. Failure to do this right will result in the single biggest stumbling block to achieving consistent profits when trading the forex market from the very start.

Would you like to find out your predominant trading style? Then take this short quiz to find out what kind of trader you are. Once you find out which category you belong to, the next step is to select the right trading strategy that flows with your personality and current lifestyle.

Are you ready? Then let's go!

 WHAT KIND OF TRADER ARE YOU?

Answer these 25 questions as accurately as possible to find out.

1. At a social event, do you:
   a. Find your best friend as soon as possible.
   b. Move around and interact with as many people as possible.
   c. Look out for interesting and popular people/groups.
   d. Sit in one corner and wait for people to talk to you.
   e. Find a group of friends and join in the conversation.

2. How often would you like to trade?
   a. A few times a week
   b. A few times a day
   c. A few times a month
   d. More than 10 times a day
   e. A fixed time every day

3. If you could have it your way, what would you be?
   a. Formula 1 racing driver
   b. Accountant
   c. Research analyst
   d. Doctor
   e. Professional chess player

4. Your favorite band releases a new album. How would you get a copy?
   a. Plan a day to visit your favorite CD shop and get a copy.
   b. Order it online.
   c. Check around for any special promotion.
   d. Download it immediately via the Internet.
   e. Wait for a friend to buy it and borrow theirs.

5. You are in a long GBP/USD trade. You watch the news and discover that a famous fund manager is in a short GBP/USD trade. You:
   a. Shift your stop loss to entry price and proceed to short GBP/USD.
   b. Stick to your trading plan.
   c. Start to research on CNBC and Bloomberg for any news concerning GBP and USD currencies.
   d. Close your existing order immediately and short GBP/USD.
   e. Change the channel to watch a movie.

6. You ride past a motorcycle showroom. You:
   a. Ask the salesperson which models are on sale.
   b. Decide to test ride a model you like.
   c. Stop and take a quick glance.
   d. Study the brochure for specifications.
   e. Continue riding on.

7. Which sport helps you to unwind?
   a. Bungee jumping
   b. Basketball
   c. Golf
   d. You prefer watching sports to unwind
   e. Tennis

8. How do you keep up with your social circle?
   a. Write on their Facebook wall
   b. Hang out with the same group once a week
   c. Maintaining your social circle is not your priority
   d. Meet up several times a year
   e. Call them up regularly for a chat

9. You love a lifestyle that:
   a. Offers a change only once in a while.
   b. Doesn't disrupt your daily schedule of doing nothing.
   c. Follows a fixed routine.
   d. Packs your time with action and activities.
   e. Throws regular challenges at you.

10. Someone cuts you off while driving. How do you typically respond?
    a. You continue driving as per normal.
    b. You step on the accelerator with your blood boiling and cut the driver off.
    c. You steam quietly in your seat.
    d. You flash your lights and toot the horn.
    e. You take a deep breath and brush it off.

11. You are waiting for a special date in a restaurant. You:
    a. Order a glass of water and update your Facebook status.
    b. Glance at your watch every three seconds.
    c. Sit quietly and prepare for an enchanted evening.
    d. Take out your seven-point checklist and tick off point 1.
    e. Check that the table is set perfectly.

12. When you capture photos with your camera, you:
    a. Take one shot and edit the picture to make it nicer.
    b. Don't really care about the picture quality.
    c. Adjust your position to get the best possible angle and lighting.
    d. Always ensure that the flash is on.
    e. Snap the shot a few times to ensure good quality.

13. Your primary reason for trading is:
    a. To beat inflation.
    b. Because you love the adrenaline rush when clicking the mouse.
    c. To earn a second income.
    d. To build up a sizable nest egg.
    e. To follow a fixed set of rules every day.

14. You pass by a political group giving a speech. You:
    a. Continue walking.
    b. Listen attentively to what they are saying.
    c. Make a note to watch the uploaded video on You Tube.
    d. Pause and listen for 15 seconds.
    e. Join the rally and make your voice heard.

15. You won the top prize in a lottery. You:
    a. Check your number to reconfirm.
    b. Jump up and celebrate.
    c. Return to the same shop and purchase another ticket.
    d. Collect your prize next week.
    e. Hold an extravagant celebration for family and friends.

16. You have to present a new project idea to your boss. You:
    a. Print out two copies of the 20-page proposal that you prepared in advance.
    b. Speak in point form with animated body language.
    c. Follow a standard template from your previous company.
    d. Draw it out on the whiteboard.
    e. Bring out the main points and emphasize the advantages.

17. What type of music do you love?
    a. Heavy metal
    b. Sentimental
    c. Classical
    d. Rock and roll
    e. No preference

18. Your idea of a vacation is:
    a. A shopping trip to Champs Elysees in Paris.
    b. A heart-thumping trip to Six Flags amusement park in the United States.
    c. A spiritual trip in India.
    d. A spa trip in Bali.
    e. The same place you enjoyed visiting last time.

19. You learn better by:
    a. Practicing past years' assessments.
    b. Researching at home alone.
    c. Asking a lot of questions.
    d. Studying with a friend.
    e. Group discussion with other people.

20. The following word describes your nature:
    a. Excitable
    b. Temperamental
    c. Calm
    d. Predictable
    e. Satisfied

21. You spot a promoter who's giving out a $10 free gift in exchange for your contact details. You:
    a. Rush to get two gifts with your wife's details as well.
    b. Whip out your mobile phone and pretend to call someone.
    c. Smile/nod at the promoter and say "No, thanks."
    d. Walk calmly and avoid any eye contact.
    e. Stop to view the gift and check if you need it first.

22. When your boss scolds you, you:
    a. Think the boss has had a bad day.
    b. Get upset and flustered.
    c. Make a note to improve.
    d. Analyze the speech and think of your retort.
    e. Pretend to listen.

23. Someone knocks on your door and asks for a donation. You:
    a. Ask what the minimum donation amount is.
    b. Get your sister to open the door to deal with it.
    c. Ask more about the donation and verify its particulars before deciding.
    d. Donate $10 without hesitation.
    e. Invite the person in for a drink to learn more about the donation.

24. You take a ride in your friend's new Porsche. He floors the pedal and hits 125 miles (200 kilometers) per hour. You:
    a. Ask him to slow down.
    b. Warn him of potential dangers along the way.
    c. Sit back and enjoy the scenery.
    d. Tell yourself this will be the last ride in your friend's car.
    e. Turn up the music and bob away ecstatically.

25. What comes to your mind as you answer all these questions?
    a. Are these the only questions?
    b. I wonder which category I'll fall into?
    c. I'll probably repeat the assessment and answer some questions differently.
    d. I wish the options were only limited to true or false.
    e. Just tell me what kind of trader I am already!

Tally up your points using this table:

Questions	A	B	C	D	E
1	5	1	3	4	2
2	3	2	4	1	5
3	1	5	3	2	4
4	2	5	3	1	4
5	2	5	3	1	4
6	2	1	4	3	5
7	1	2	4	5	3
8	1	3	5	4	2
9	3	4	5	1	2
10	5	1	3	2	4
11	3	1	4	5	2
12	4	1	3	5	2
13	4	1	3	2	5
14	5	2	3	4	1
15	3	2	5	4	1
16	4	1	5	2	3
17	1	3	4	2	5
18	2	1	4	3	5

(Continued)

Questions	A	B	C	D	E
19	5	4	1	3	2
20	2	1	4	5	3
21	1	5	3	4	2
22	3	1	4	2	5
23	1	3	2	5	4
24	3	2	4	5	1
25	4	2	3	5	1

Total Score:

Scorecard

25–34: Scalper

You are a true-blue scalper. You like to have fun and variety is the name of the game. You get bored easily, which is why you live a life filled with activities. As an individual, you are not afraid to be original or contrarian. However, you display a mildly aggressive nature when things don't go your way.

You like the excitement of fast-moving markets, and you don't like it when trades take too long to exit. Your ability to focus on the charts for several hours at a time is an important part of your success.

Impatience stands out as one of your characteristics, because you expect your trades to become profitable immediately. As a scalper, impatience can work in your favor too, because you will exit trades promptly if they go against you. Additionally, this quick-thinking helps you to maintain a flexible mind-set when setting up new trades in the opposite direction when the need calls for it.

35–46: Scalper/Day Trader

You are an excitable and passionate individual. You are a person who does not do well with details as your current lifestyle does not have a fixed routine yet. As a scalper/day trader, you embody characteristics in both categories. Sometimes you love the action when markets are moving fast. At other times, you tend to get stressed in the same market conditions.

Due to your time flexibility, on some days you can commit several hours looking at the charts. However, on days when your schedule fills up, you can only afford to glance at the charts for several minutes each time. You like to vary your trading style according to the time you have. When time permits, you prefer to spend hours looking at the charts and scalp, taking a few pips each time. When time is a factor, you prefer to pick the best trade setup for that day.

You are extremely delighted when your trade registers a profit, but your mood sours considerably when you hit a loss. The good news is that when you are wrong, you don't have a problem owning up to it. As part of your personality, you like to experiment with different trading strategies and systems to keep your interest from waning.

47–56: Day Trader

You are a true-blue day trader. You like to keep abreast of news and watch the markets for any moves throughout the day. As a tech-savvy individual, you love your gadgets and probably own at least a laptop, a tablet, and a smart phone. These devices help you to stay on top of the markets. Analytical and unbiased, you take pride in crunching the numbers after you have done your research and data mining.

Sometimes you take it a step further and calculate all possible scenarios and outcomes for each trade before triggering it. You are not afraid of risk. In fact, one of your strengths lies in effective risk management because you might have a couple of open trades in a day. You are not known for reckless trading, but at odd times you throw caution to the wind and enter a trade when not all the rules have been met. During those times, you find it difficult to cut your losses because of your nature to defend your decisions.

The great part about you is that you like to face and solve challenges. Life is an adventure, and you look forward to new things every day. Your zest reveals your personality as an individual who does not allow problems to weigh you down.

57–68: Day/Swing Trader

You are an optimistic person who is dedicated to improving yourself every day. You are well-read and street-smart, and your life has pretty much settled down into a fixed routine in terms of work and play. As a busy person, you pride yourself in effective time management, and you usually keep a daily to-do list that helps you prioritize your activities. Due to your working hours, you are content to take a smaller number of trades daily or weekly.

You like to plan ahead, and the main reason for you starting to trade is to build up a second income to complement your active income. Occasionally, when you have some spare time, you tend to overanalyze your trade setups. This sometimes results in a tendency to abandon your game plan because you are swayed by different sources of information.

69–78: Swing Trader

You are a true-blue swing trader. Your day job takes up most of your time, but you enjoy trading on the side. In fact, because of your lack of time, you actually like it that you don't have to analyze the market too much.

You are comfortable to sit and wait for the best trade setup and are not at all bothered with how prices fluctuate during the day. In fact, you know too well that too much time spent looking at the charts can bring about the danger of emotional trading.

You classify yourself as a conservative person who doesn't enjoy taking unnecessary risks. Unlike most traders, who don't have a trading plan, you thrive on having a solid trading plan. Rules are clearly defined, and you know exactly when to enter and exit a trade.

Once you decide on a trade, you are not easily swayed to change it. You are perfectly fine to see your trade fluctuate between profit and loss, as your main concern is whether you followed all the rules and executed the trade correctly. Your eye is firmly fixed on a favorable risk to reward ratio.

The best thing that you like about forex trading is that it doesn't cause you to alter your lifestyle. After all, when you execute a couple of trades a week, the result is a steady increase in part-time income.

79–90: Swing/Position Trader
You are an independent thinker who ignores popular opinion. As a rational and practical individual, you make your own decisions after taking in all the relevant information. You are fully aware that frequent trading leads to more mistakes. Hence, you adjust your trading style to take fewer trades with bigger gains. An avid reader of the markets, you have a good grasp of the fundamentals and how countries are managing their economies.

However, your depth and insights on the markets can sometimes be a double-edged sword. Due to your analysis of mid- to long-term trends, procrastination sometimes can set in. This keeps you from executing the trade even though all the rules have been met.

If left unchecked, your procrastination can slowly take root in your character. You now tend to look for more reasons to substantiate each trade entry, or lack thereof. This vicious cycle can affect your trading style if you don't take steps to rectify it.

97–100: Position Trader
You are a true-blue position trader. You are a calm soul who's sensitive to feelings and don't enjoy conflict. As an individual, you are more intuitive than analytical. Stress is a foreign word because you don't have much of it in your life. You are able to detach any emotional highs and lows you experience in trading.

Due to your trading style, you prefer to trade with a large account size to help you weather fluctuations of hundreds or even thousands of pips. You hardly ever look at technicals as your main focus is on the fundamentals of how governments run their countries.

You are able to see the big picture of how monetary policies and fiscal policies affect currency movements farther down the road. Your biggest virtue is patience, as you don't mind waiting several weeks or months for your reward.

101 and above: Mechanical Trader
You are a true-blue mechanical trader. You like routine and structure in life. Sometimes, eating your favorite food every day for a week makes you happy.

As a newbie in the forex market, you get overwhelmed with all the information out there. You want to get started, but you're just not sure how. Hence, you depend on a robust system to help you make educated decisions. The system you settle for either requires you to spend a few minutes a day to trigger the trade or trades on its own via automated software.

You have tried to make sense of the news that impacts the market, but that has been the cause of your stress. This is because you realize that news occurs on a daily basis, and you either can't keep up with it or you don't want to do so.

News is the main reason you have a love-hate relationship with the forex market. You know that fundamental news causes the prices to move, but you can't manage the unpredictable way in which it does. You settle for a trading methodology that disregards the impact of news. Doing this takes the stress out of trading and puts the focus on delivering a style that is both profitable and system driven.

SUMMARY

The perfect strategy to use in the forex market is the one that perfectly suits you. Two traders can employ the exact same strategy but have different results. This is mainly due to the trader's personality, which causes him or her to meddle with the trade as it is engaged.

There are essentially five categories of traders in the world: scalpers, day traders, swing traders, position traders, and mechanical traders. The main difference among the categories of traders is the time frames employed while trading.

Essentially, the length of time in which a trading position is held increases from a scalper to a day trader, to a swing trader, and finally to a position trader. Mechanical traders are oblivious to the passing of time. Their trades are based on a fixed routine, regardless of time frame and regardless of market activity.

No one category of traders is better than the other, as each category has its own unique characteristics and advantages. The end goal for all categories of traders is the same: to be consistently profitable when trading the forex market.

Just as sports coaches put athletes through a series of tests to ascertain their dominant strengths, budding forex traders must determine their own strengths. Finding your flow as a trader is critical to your goal of becoming a profitable trader once and for all.

PART TWO

Strategies to Win
the Game

This part is divided into five chapters. Each chapter covers strategies for the five profiles of scalper, day trader, swing trader, position trader, and mechanical trader.

Chapter 6 covers two strategies for scalpers, called the rapid fire and the piranha. These strategies are used on the lowest time frames, namely the minute chart and the 5-minute chart.

Chapter 7 covers four strategies for day traders. The first two strategies are focused on breakouts while the next two are centered purely on trading the news. A unique way of trading the news, called the Rule of 20, is also discussed here. All four strategies are employed using the 15-minute and 30-minute time frame.

Chapter 8 covers five strategies for swing traders. As swing traders typically exit their positions within two to five days, the time frames used for the strategies are longer than the day traders. Hence, all five of the swing trading strategies are used on the hourly and the 4-hourly time frame.

Chapter 9 covers three strategies for position traders. The first one, swap and fly, takes advantage of interest rate differentials between the currencies and aims to earn maximum returns by holding on to positions for an extended period of time. The next two strategies are used specifically for the two most popular commodities in the world: oil and gold.

Chapter 10 covers three strategies for mechanical traders. Traders in this category are oblivious to the passing of time. This is why all strategies discussed here employ three different time frames from the other categories: the 5-minute chart, the 15-minute chart, and the daily chart.

ABOUT THE WEBSITE

Please check www.wiley.com/go/17strategies for more examples of the strategies found in the next five chapters. Refer to the About the Website page at the end of this book for more information.

FXPRIMUS 100% BONUS TRADING CREDIT

Get a 100% Forex Trading Bonus and Then Withdraw It
Just fund USD100 or more in your Live FXPRIMUS Forex account to qualify.

Examples:
- Fund USD100 and get USD200 to trade with.
- Fund USD500 and get USD1,000 to trade with.
- Fund USD1,000 and get USD2,000 to trade with.

Fund any amount between USD100 and USD10,000 to receive your corresponding 100% bonus trading credit. The more you fund, the bigger your bonus trading credit.

Visit www.wiley.com/go/17strategies for more details.

Terms and conditions apply.

CHAPTER 6

Strategies for Scalpers

A s a scalper, you love strategies characterized by high-volume trading. These strategies are designed to enter the market frequently, taking small profits each time.

Most scalping strategies employ either indicators (including custom indicators) or price action (including candlestick patterns) or a combination of both. Ideally, the strategies should be employed on the lowest time frames available on the broker's platform.

The two scalping techniques discussed here—rapid fire and piranha—are developed on the M1 (1-minute) and M5 (5-minute) charts respectively. These two time frames give you ample opportunities to enter in and out of the market several times a day. Although scalping can be very exciting, the constant monitoring of market movements can give rise to fatigue and loss of focus.

Hence, you need to know when to take a break or call it a day. Failure to do so could result in unwarranted mistakes. To overcome this, establish simple guidelines or rules for yourself.

As an example, say: "I will take a break after trading for one hour" or "I will stop trading after I hit my daily target of 20 pips."

Remember, overtrading does not necessarily yield more profits. As a scalper, your most important tools are a very reliable computer, a high-speed Internet connection, and a pot of coffee to help you stay awake.

STRATEGY 1: RAPID-FIRE STRATEGY

The rapid-fire strategy was designed with two criteria in mind:

1. The most liquid currency pair in the world
2. The lowest time frame available

This criterion led to the development of the strategy on the minute chart (M1) for the EUR/USD currency pair.

The M1 time frame is fast-paced and exhilarating. If you are not careful, the adrenaline rush you experience can cloud your trading decisions. This problem is compounded by the high frequency of trading opportunities that the strategy presents. On average, there are about 30 to 40 trading opportunities for the rapid-fire strategy every day.

This is the reason why the rapid-fire strategy employs two indicators to assist you in spotting objective trades throughout the day. You can then fire off the trade rapidly once you decide to take it.

Time Frame

The rapid-fire strategy works with the 1-minute (M1) time frame. Each candlestick on the chart represents 1 minute of price movement.

Indicators

We use these indicators for the rapid-fire strategy:

1. Parabolic SAR with default setting:
   a. Step 0.02
   b. Maximum 0.2
2. Simple moving average (SMA), period 60, and apply to close.

Parabolic SAR The "step" is also known as the acceleration factor (AF), and it starts at a minimum value of 0.02. Maximum 0.2 means that the AF can reach a maximum of 0.2, no matter how long the uptrend or downtrend extends. A higher step basically moves the SAR closer to the price action, which makes a reversal more likely. If the step is set too high, the indicator reverses often and produces whipsaws.

The Parabolic SAR is an indicator developed by J. Welles Wilder to find trends in market prices. The acronym "SAR" stands for "stop and reverse."

$$SAR(i) = SAR(i - 1) + AF \times \{EPRICE - SAR(i - 1)\}$$

Where:

SAR (i) = the value of the indicator on the current bar;
SAR(i − 1) = the value of the indicator on the previous bar;

AF = the acceleration factor. This factor is increased by 0.02 each time a new EPRICE is recorded.

EPRICE (Extreme Price) = the highest price reached during the current uptrend or the lowest price during a downtrend. In each trend, when the price reaches a new high or low, the EPRICE will be updated to that value.

Traders utilize the positions of the Parabolic SAR to generate buy or sell signals. A bullish signal is generated when the dots of the Parabolic SAR is below the price, causing traders to expect the upward momentum to continue. Conversely, a bearish signal is generated when the dot is above the price, causing traders to expect the downward momentum to continue.

The indicator works extremely well when markets are moving in a trend.

Simple Moving Average 60 A simple moving average (SMA) is calculated by adding the price of the candlestick over a given number of periods and then dividing this total sum by the number of periods. Since this strategy uses minute candlesticks, SMA 60 (apply to close) is the sum of closing prices for 60 candles divided by 60. The figures are dynamic, which means that old data are dropped as new ones are added. This rolling figure causes the moving average to move along the time scale.

The most common use of the SMA is to identify the direction of market momentum. When the market price is above the moving average, the market is deemed to have a bullish momentum and traders will look for an entry to go long. When the market price is below the moving average, the market is deemed to have a bearish momentum and traders will look for an entry to go short.

Currency Pairs

The strategy is designed specifically for the EUR/USD, the most traded currency pair in the world.

Strategy Concept

The strategy concept is a trend-scalping strategy, which means it works best in a trend. The strategy combines two trend indicators, SMA 60 and

Parabolic SAR with default setting (step 0.02). The SMA 60 is used to identify the direction of the momentum. This means that we look to long EUR/USD when the price is above the SMA 60. Similarly, we look to short EUR/USD when the price is below the SMA 60.

The Parabolic SAR is used to give the exact entry signal for both long and short positions. When the price for EUR/USD goes above the Parabolic SAR, we fire off a long trade. When the price for EUR/USD goes below the Parabolic SAR, we fire off a short trade.

Long Trade Setup

Here are the steps to execute a long trade using the rapid-fire strategy:

1. Look for the market price to go above the SMA 60.
2. Wait for the Parabolic SAR to move above the market price.
3. Once the market price goes above the Parabolic SAR, the Parabolic SAR will appear below the market price. This is the signal to enter for long. (See Figure 6.1.)
4. The stop loss is set at 15 pips below the entry price.
5. The profit target is set at 10 pips above the entry price. (See Figure 6.2.)

FIGURE 6.1 Parabolic SAR Appears Below Market Price

FIGURE 6.2 Set Profit Target 10 Pips Above Entry Price

From the long example in Figure 6.3:

$$\text{Entry price} = 1.2934$$
$$\text{Stop loss} = 1.2919$$
$$\text{Profit target} = 1.2944$$

The risk for this trade is 15 pips, and the reward is 10 pips. The risk to reward ratio is 1.5:1, which yields a 2% return if we take a 3% risk.

FIGURE 6.3 Trade Hits Profit Target

Short Trade Setup

Here are the steps to execute a short trade using the rapid-fire strategy:

1. Look for the market price to go below the SMA 60.
2. Wait for the Parabolic SAR to move below the market price.
3. Once the market price goes below the Parabolic SAR, the Parabolic SAR will appear above the market price. This is the signal to enter for short. (See Figure 6.4.)
4. Set the stop loss at 15 pips above the entry price.
5. Set the profit target at 10 pips below the entry price. (See Figure 6.5.)

From the short example in Figure 6.6:

$$\text{Entry price} = 1.2937$$
$$\text{Stop loss} = 1.2952$$
$$\text{Profit target} = 1.2927$$

The risk for this trade is 15 pips, and the reward is 10 pips. The risk to reward ratio is 1.5:1, which yields a 2% return if we take a 3% risk.

FIGURE 6.4 Parabolic SAR Appears Above the Market Price

FIGURE 6.5 Set Profit Target 10 Pips Below Entry Price

FIGURE 6.6 Trade Hits Profit Target

Strategy Roundup

The rapid-fire strategy could give you another trade signal even before the current trade exits. It is not uncommon to encounter consecutive trading signals one after the other, simply because of the low time frame used.

As a scalper, you have to decide how to manage the trades, especially when the setups come fast and furious. Do you exit the previous trade before entering a new one, ignore any new trade signals until the current trade exits, or simply fire off whenever there is a trade signal?

Remember, the rapid-fire strategy works best in a trending environment. It requires fast thinking and nimble reactions. It is most suitable for action-driven traders who can maintain their composure while in the thick of action.

STRATEGY 2: PIRANHA STRATEGY

The forex market spends most of its time either in a trend or in a range. The rapid-fire scalping strategy works best in a trend. The piranha strategy was developed to work when markets move in a range.

Let us get right into the world of the piranhas. Piranhas take small frequent bites off their prey until it is totally devoured. Although a single bite may not cause much harm, the frequency of the bites causes the attack to be deadly. In much the same way, the piranha strategy was developed to give scalpers ample opportunities to bite the market and chew off small profits each time.

This strategy is designed specifically for the GBP/USD currency pair, using the 5-minute (M5) time frame. On average, there are about 15 to 20 trading opportunities for the piranha strategy every day.

Time Frame

The piranha strategy works with the 5-minute (M5) time frame. This means that each candlestick on the chart represents 5 minutes of price movement.

Indicators

We use this indicator for the piranha strategy:

One set of Bollinger Bands
a. Period 12, Shift 0.
b. Deviation 2 (default).

Developed by technical trader John Bollinger, Bollinger Bands consist of three lines, with the simple moving average in the center and the outer Bands plotted using standard deviation formula away from the simple moving average.

Standard deviation is a measure of price volatility. When markets become more volatile, the Bands widen and move farther from the center moving average line. The formulas to calculate the upper and lower Bands are:

$$\text{Upper band} = \text{SMA} + (\text{D} \times \text{Std Dev})$$
$$\text{Lower band} = \text{SMA} - (\text{D} \times \text{Std Dev})$$

Where:

SMA = Simple moving average

D = Deviation value (e.g., 1, 2, 3, etc.)

Std Dev = Standard deviation

Due to the complexity of the formula, I will not focus too much on it; instead, I focus more on the significance of the upper and lower Bands.

When prices approach the upper band, it is considered to be in an overbought region. When prices approach the lower band, it is considered oversold. At these extreme levels, markets tend to consolidate and move back to the center moving average line.

By setting a higher deviation value, the price volatility measure will be magnified, and you will get a Bollinger band with wider upper and lower Bands.

Currency Pairs

The strategy is designed for the cable, which is the nickname for the currency pair GBP/USD.

Strategy Concept

Bollinger Bands are used to identify the trading band of the GBP/USD. The Bands help us to mimic the nature of the piranhas by giving objective entries for long and short positions. (See Figure 6.7.)

Long trades are taken when market prices touch the bottom band; short trades are taken when market prices touch the upper band.

Piranhas are active in relatively calm waters, such as rivers, but not in the rough open seas with strong currents and waves. In much the same way, avoid trading this strategy at times of major news releases during the U.S. and U.K. trading hours, as such environments reflect the rough open seas with strong currents and waves. We use the GBP/USD currency pair on the M5 time frame to illustrate both long and short trades.

FIGURE 6.7 Bollinger Bands Used for Piranha Strategy

Candlestick touches
lower band

FIGURE 6.8 Candlestick Touches Lower Band of Bollinger Bands

Long Trade Setup

Here are the steps to execute a long trade using the piranha strategy:

1. Wait for the market to touch the lower band of the Bollinger Bands.
2. Enter for a long when the market price touches the lower band of the Bollinger Bands. (See Figure 6.8.)

3. Set the stop loss at 10 pips below the entry price.

4. Set the profit target at 5 pips above the entry price. (See Figure 6.9)

From the long example in Figure 6.10:

$$Entry\ price = 1.5931$$
$$Stop\ loss = 1.5921$$
$$Profit\ target = 1.5936$$

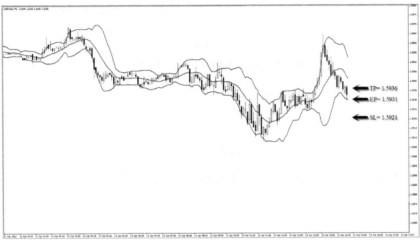

FIGURE 6.9 Set Profit Target 5 Pips Above Entry Price

FIGURE 6.10 Trade Hits Profit Target

The risk for this trade is 10 pips, and the reward is 5 pips. The risk to reward ratio is 2:1, which yields us a 1.5% return if we take a 3% risk.

Short Trade Setup

Here are the steps to execute a short trade using the piranha strategy:

1. Wait for the market to touch the upper band of the Bollinger Bands.
2. Enter for a short when the market touches the upper band of the Bollinger Bands. (See Figure 6.11.)
3. Set the stop loss at 10 pips above the entry price.
4. Set the profit target at 5 pips below the entry price. (See Figure 6.12.)

From the short example in Figure 6.13:

$$\text{Entry price} = 1.5941$$
$$\text{Stop loss} = 1.5951$$
$$\text{Profit target} = 1.5936$$

The risk for this trade is 10 pips, and the reward is 5 pips. The risk to reward ratio is 2:1, which yields us a 1.5% return if we take a 3% risk.

FIGURE 6.11   Candlestick Touches Upper Band of Bollinger Bands

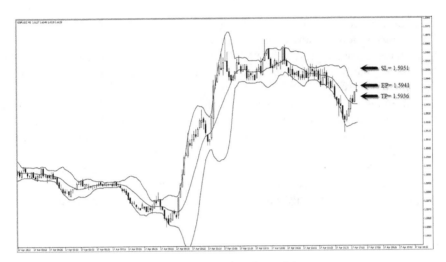

FIGURE 6.12 Set Profit Target 5 Pips Below Entry Price
Source: Created with FX Primus Ltd, a PRIME Mantle Corporation PLC company. All rights reserved.

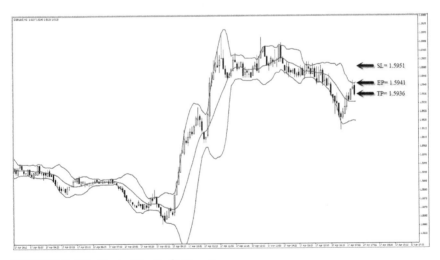

FIGURE 6.13 Trade Hits Profit Target
Source: Created with FX Primus Ltd, a PRIME Mantle Corporation PLC company. All rights reserved.

Strategy Roundup

At the beginning of this section, I mentioned that piranhas attack their prey until it is totally devoured. In much the same way, once your trade hits a stop loss, the loss is telling you that there is nothing left of your prey and it's time to look for a new one.

Hence, hitting a stop loss is a telltale sign that the market is no longer trading in a band and it is starting to move into a trend. So how do you look for the next prey?

The answer is to look for a trade that is in the opposite direction of your stop-loss trade. For example, if you took a long trade that resulted in a stop loss, look to short the GBP/USD at the next opportunity with the same rules.

This is an important consideration and a neat trick for you to navigate yourself in trending markets. As this strategy was designed primarily for range trading, it fails badly when the market goes into a strong trend.

CHAPTER 7

Strategies for Day Traders

As a day trader, your biggest pet peeve is holding trading positions overnight. You are more concerned with finishing the day without an open position than the actual result of the trade itself.

Your trades are characterized by profit targets of around 20 to 50 pips per trade. Most day trading strategies involve a combination of both technical and fundamental analysis.

For technical analysis, chart patterns, candlestick patterns, and indicators are important considerations. For fundamental analysis, trading important news, such as non-farm payrolls (NFP) and interest rates, is the focus.

Four strategies are discussed in this section. The first two—fade the break and trade the break—are centered on technical analysis. The next two—gawk the talk and balk the talk—are centered on fundamental analysis, or news trading.

All strategies are developed using the 15-minute (M15) time frame and the 30-minute (M30) time frame. The biggest reason why these time frames are most suited for day traders is because the positions are most likely to exit in a day. As a day trader, the biggest frustration that you will face is the constant dilemma of leaving a trade open or exiting it manually. Sometimes, Murphy's Law strikes when you decide to exit the trade manually, sending your trade to its intended profit level had you left it open in the first place.

To prevent such scenarios, set some guidelines for yourself when it comes to closing off your open positions. An example could be "I will close off my position exactly at 11 P.M. every day, regardless of the trading result." An objective rule like that can help you to manage your positions better—and prevent Murphy's Law from striking in the future.

STRATEGY 3: FADE THE BREAK

The forex market is a constant battle between bulls and bears. Sometimes this fight occurs between retail and institutional traders. It is common knowledge that institutional traders prey on unassuming retail traders who sometimes engage in emotional trading.

Fade the break is a strategy that follows the trail of the institutional traders. It allows retail traders like you and me to pick up the clues of the smart money. Let's get right into it.

Time Frame

The fade the break strategy works with the 15-minute (M15) or 30-minute (M30) candle. This means that each candle on the chart represents 15 or 30 minutes of price movement.

Indicators

No indicators are used for this strategy. We use support and resistance levels only.

Currency Pairs

This strategy is suitable for all currency pairs listed on the broker's platform, especially the seven major currency pairs of:

EUR/USD
USD/JPY
GBP/USD
USD/CHF
USD/CAD
AUD/USD
NZD/USD

Strategy Concept

Markets often reverse after a failure to break above the resistance level or below the support level. At the resistance level, the failure is characterized by the shadow of the candle that goes above the resistance level but fails to close above it. Subsequently the price falls back below the resistance level.

At the support level, the failure is characterized by the shadow of the candle that goes below the support level but fails to close below it. Subsequently the price rises above the support level.

Many retail traders get caught at exactly these levels because they take the "break" of the resistance as a signal that prices will continue to go up. Similarly, they assume that the break of the support is a signal that prices will continue to move down. Let's see how to trade this setup when it occurs.

Long Trade Setup

We use the EUR/USD on the M30 time frame to illustrate long trades. Here are the steps to execute the fade the break strategy for long:

1. Identify the support level.
2. Identify a candle that has a shadow that goes below the support level.
3. Wait for that candle to close as a bull candle. This is called the false-break candle. (See Figure 7.1.)
4. Enter at the opening of the next candle.
5. Set a stop loss of 5 pips below the low price of the false break candle.
6. Set two profit targets for this trade. Set the two targets at a risk to reward ratio of 1:1 and 1:2 respectively. (See Figure 7.2.)

FIGURE 7.1   False-Break Candlestick

FIGURE 7.2   Enter at Opening of Next Candle

FIGURE 7.3   Trade Hits Profit Targets

7. In this example, the stop loss is 28 pips, the first profit target is 28 pips from the entry price, and the second profit target is 56 pips from the entry price.

From the long example in Figure 7.3:

$$\text{Entry price} = 1.3090$$
$$\text{Stop loss} = 1.3062$$

Profit target 1 = 1.3118
Proft target 2 = 1.3146

The risk for this trade is 28 pips, and the reward is 56 pips if both targets are hit. The risk to reward ratio is 1:2, which yields a tidy 6% return if we take a 3% risk.

Short Trade Setup

We use the GBP/USD on the M15 time frame to illustrate short trades. Here are the steps to execute the fade the break strategy for short:

1. Identify the resistance level.
2. Identify a candle that has a shadow that goes above the resistance level.
3. Wait for that candle to close as a bear candle. This is called the false-break candle. (See Figure 7.4.)

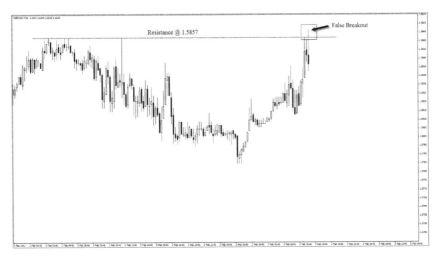

FIGURE 7.4   False-Break Candlestick

Source: Created with FX Primus Ltd, a PRIME Mantle Corporation PLC company. All rights reserved.

4. Enter at the opening of the next candle.
5. Set a stop loss of 5 pips above the high price of the false-break candle.
6. Set two profit targets for this trade. Set the two targets at a risk to reward ratio of 1:1 and 1:2 respectively. (See Figure 7.5.)
7. In this example, the stop loss is 22 pips, the first profit target is 22 pips from the entry price, and the second profit target is 44 pips from the entry price.

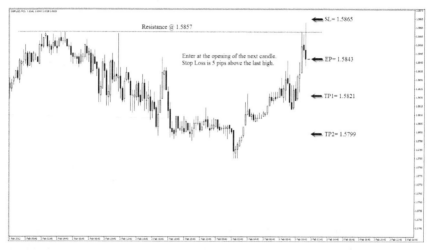

FIGURE 7.5 Enter at Opening of Next Candlestick
Source: Created with FX Primus Ltd, a PRIME Mantle Corporation PLC company. All rights reserved.

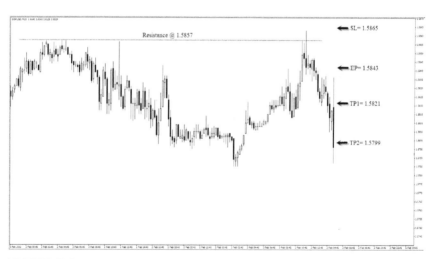

FIGURE 7.6 Trade Hits Profit Targets
Source: Created with FX Primus Ltd, a PRIME Mantle Corporation PLC company. All rights reserved.

From the short example in Figure 7.6:

Entry price = 1.5843
Stop loss = 1.5865
Profit target 1 = 1.5821
Proft target 2 = 1.5799

The risk for this trade is 22 pips, and the reward is 44 pips if both targets are hit. The risk to reward ratio is 1:2, which yields a tidy 6% return if we take a 3% risk.

Strategy Roundup

The main reason why false breaks occur is due to the tussle between retail and institutional traders. Both groups of traders easily identify levels of support and resistance, and false breaks are big clues for us retail traders that there is a lack of momentum to push prices further.

Remember that false breaks are traps to catch day traders off guard. However, fade the break helps us to turn these traps into opportunities.

STRATEGY 4: TRADE THE BREAK

In the previous strategy, we discussed a method to trade the market when prices fail to close above resistance or below support. In trade the break, we see exactly where to place our entries and exits for both short and long positions. The biggest difference between trade the break and fade the break is that for trade the break, prices have to close above resistance or below support.

For this strategy, the trick is not so much in the entry price but in the stop loss. Many retail traders have no problem identifying areas of entry since the directional bias is to follow the momentum. However, the correct placement of the stop loss is what separates winners from losers.

You see, as with the previous fade the break strategy, both retail and institutional traders closely watch areas of support and resistance. More often than not, these areas are the biggest battlegrounds between these two groups of traders. This is why prices sometimes reverse quickly once they break above resistance or below support.

When we learn how to place the stop loss correctly for these trades, many potential "losers" can in fact turn into winners. Let's get right into it.

Time Frame

Trade the break works with the 15-minute (M15) or 30-minute (M30) candle. This means that each candle on the chart represents 15 minutes or 30 minutes of price movement.

Indicators

No indicators are used for this strategy.

Currency Pairs

This strategy is suitable for all currency pairs listed on the broker's platform, especially the seven major currency pairs of:

EUR/USD

USD/JPY

GBP/USD

USD/CHF

USD/CAD

AUD/USD

NZD/USD

Strategy Concept

Trade the break is all about momentum. A big clue is seen when prices close above resistance or below support. This clue tells us that momentum is building strongly on one side. When prices close above resistance, that candle is called the breakout candle. A long trade is then taken at the opening price of the next candle. The stop loss is placed below the midpoint of the prior range because we do not expect prices to fall back below that point.

When prices close below support, that candle is also called the breakout candle. A short trade is then taken at the opening price of the next candle. The stop loss is placed above the midpoint of the prior range because we do not expect prices to rise above that point.

Long Trade Setup

We use the AUD/USD on M15 time frame to illustrate long trades. Here are the steps to execute the trade the break strategy for long:

1. Use at least two lows and two highs to identify the support and resistance levels. (See Figure 7.7.)
2. Identify a candle that closes above the resistance. This is the breakout candle. (See Figure 7.8.)
3. Enter long at the opening of the next candle.
4. Set the stop loss at the 60% mark of the range (distance between the support and resistance) below the resistance. In this example, the distance between the support and resistance is 41 pips; the stop loss is set at 25 pips below the resistance.

FIGURE 7.7 Use Two Lows and Two Highs to Identify Support and Resistance Levels
Source: Created with FX Primus Ltd, a PRIME Mantle Corporation PLC company. All rights reserved.

FIGURE 7.8 Identify a Candle that Closes Above Resistance
Source: Created with FX Primus Ltd, a PRIME Mantle Corporation PLC company. All rights reserved.

5. Set two profit targets for this trade. The targets are set at a risk to reward ratio of 1:1 and 1:2 respectively. Since the stop loss is 44 pips (distance between the EP and the SL), the first profit target will be 44 pips, and the second profit target will be 88 pips. (See Figure 7.9.)

FIGURE 7.9   Profit Targets for This Trade

FIGURE 7.10   Trade Hits Profit Targets

From the long example in Figure 7.10:

$$\text{Entry price} = 1.0351$$
$$\text{Stop loss} = 1.0307$$
$$\text{Profit target 1} = 1.0395$$
$$\text{Proft target 2} = 1.0439$$

The risk for this trade is 44 pips, and the reward is 88 pips if both targets are hit. The risk to reward ratio is 1:2, which yields a tidy 6% return if we take a 3% risk.

Short Trade Setup

We use the AUD/USD on M15 time frame for illustrating short trades. Here are the steps to execute the trade the break strategy for short:

1. Use at least two lows and two highs to identify the support and resistance levels. (See Figure 7.11.)
2. Identify a candle that closes below the support. This is the breakout candle. (See Figure 7.12.)
3. Enter short at the opening of the next candle.
4. Set the stop loss at the 60% mark of the range (distance between the support and resistance) above the support. In this example, the distance between the support and resistance is 42 pips; the stop loss is set at 26 pips above the support.
5. We set two profit targets for this trade. The targets are set at a risk to reward ratio of 1:1 and 1:2 respectively. Since the stop loss is 31 pips (distance between EP and SL), the first profit target is 31 pips, and the second profit target is 62 pips. (See Figure 7.13.)

FIGURE 7.11 Use Two Lows and Two Highs to Identify Support and Resistance Levels

Source: Created with FX Primus Ltd, a PRIME Mantle Corporation PLC company. All rights reserved.

FIGURE 7.12 Identify a Candle that Closes Below Support

FIGURE 7.13 Profit Targets Set for This Trade

From the short example in Figure 7.14:

$$Entry\ price = 1.0498$$
$$Stop\ loss = 1.0529$$
$$Profit\ target\ 1 = 1.0467$$
$$Proft\ target\ 2 = 1.0436$$

FIGURE 7.14 Trade Hits Profit Targets

Source: Created with FX Primus Ltd, a PRIME Mantle Corporation PLC company. All rights reserved.

The risk for this trade is 31 pips, and the reward is 62 pips if both targets are hit. The risk to reward ratio is 1:2, which yields a tidy 6% return if we take a 3% risk.

Strategy Roundup

As a trader, our job is not to predict but to react. In other words, we should not second-guess where the market is going and execute trades based on assumptions. Whenever the market approaches resistance or support levels, traders tend to jump in prematurely, which can yield disastrous consequences when the markets don't go the way we want.

Instead, a better option is to wait for the story to unfold. It certainly pays to wait for a confirmation before jumping onboard the breakout bandwagon. The confirmation comes in the form of the breakout candle that closes above the resistance or below the support. This is the market's way of telling us that it has enough momentum to continue the run.

By now, you must have realized that the two strategies—fade the break and trade the break—work hand in hand. Both strategies require us to pause and wait for a confirmation candle before deciding what to do. These candles are either false-break candles or breakout candles. With these two strategies, we can take a trade regardless of market direction.

TRADING THE NEWS

Trading the news is one of the best ways I know of making good profits in a short time with bearable risk. This is because volatility is highest during these announcements, and traders tend to look out for these times to capitalize on price movements for a quick profit.

If you are a trader who loves making trading decisions around news announcements, the next two strategies are for you. One of the greatest advantages of news trading is accessibility. Today, more than ever before, we are able to access the results as soon as they are released and trade off them.

Many free websites report economic news events almost hourly. The one that I use daily is a site called forexfactory.com. The site is very user friendly, and the economic calendar allows you to view the upcoming news at a glance.

The news comes with color-coded flags, with red flags signifying the greatest potential impact. I prefer trading these red flags as opposed to the orange or yellow ones because the potential for big movements is higher. These red flags are also the basis for the events discussed in the next section.

The top seven news that cause the greatest moves in the forex market are discussed next.

Interest Rates

As discussed in Chapter 2, central banks usually raise or lower interest rates to achieve a particular inflation target. If the current inflation is below their target, banks may cut the rate to entice consumers to spend more, given the cheaper borrowing rate. In this way, banks increase the demand for goods and services.

An increase in demand for goods and services would result in an increase in inflation. Conversely, banks may hike their rate if the current inflation reading is above their target. Making borrowing costs more expensive puts a curb on demand and spending and thus lowers inflation. High interest rates subsequently cause funds to flow into that particular country as compared to a country with relatively lower rates.

Key point: When a country raises interest rates, its currency tends to strengthen.

Gross Domestic Product

Gross domestic product (GDP) is considered the broadest measure of a country's economy because it represents the monetary value of all goods and services produced within a country's borders in a specific time period, usually a year. Most countries target economic growth at a rate of about 2% per year. When GDP figures are rising, demand for the nation's currency increases. This causes its currency to rise in value against other currencies. In much the same way, a decreasing GDP could mean that a country is not growing. In fact, a recession is defined as two consecutive quarters of negative growth.

Hence, lower GDP figures tend to decrease the country's value because growth is stunted and confidence is affected. This causes foreign capital to leave the country and, in turn, lowers the value of its currency against other currencies.

Key point: When GDP figures are better than expected, the currency tends to strengthen.

Employment

Employment data is highly sought after by retail traders. In the United States, this news is termed the non-farm payrolls (NFP), and it accounts for about 80% of the workers who contribute to the GDP. The NFP is released on the first Friday of every month and is arguably the most traded piece of news worldwide.

The NFP report is statistical data from the U.S. Bureau of Labor Statistics. It represents the total number of paid U.S. workers of any business, excluding:

- General government employees
- Private household employees
- Employees of nonprofit organizations that provide assistance to individuals
- Farm employees

The figures in an NFP report indicate the number of jobs created in that particular month. Increasing employment levels signal robust growth, which directly increases consumer spending and causes confidence to rise. Naturally, the added effect of consumer spending and confidence brings about demand for US dollars and causes it to rise.

An increase in unemployment levels in a country tends to signal a slowdown in growth because consumer spending falls. This slowdown impacts demand for goods and services and causes business confidence to drop as well. Even those still employed tend to worry about the future and reduce spending. As demand continues to falter, the currency supply builds up, and its value decreases against other currencies.

Key point: When employment figures are higher than expected, the currency tends to strengthen.

Trade Balance

The trade balance measures the ratio of exports to imports for a given country's economy. If exports are higher than imports (called a trade surplus), the trade balance will be positive. If imports are higher than exports (called a trade deficit), the trade balance will be negative.

Trade balance is derived primarily from three factors:

1. The price of goods in a country
2. Tax and tariff levies on imported or exported goods
3. The exchange rate between two currencies

This last factor is fundamental to forex trading. Since the trade balance depends so heavily on the current state of exchange rates between two countries, the trade balance is a key indicator of a country's economic health.

Key point: When trade balance figures are higher than expected, the currency tends to strengthen.

Consumer Price Index

The consumer price index (CPI) is the best measure of inflation for any country. It measures the change in the cost of a fixed basket of products and services, including housing, electricity, food, and transportation. The CPI is published monthly. In some countries, the CPI is called the inflation index or the cost-of-living index.

A high CPI figure shows that the inflation in a country is high. Most countries tend to keep the annual inflation rate between the 2% and 3% mark. If inflation is stubbornly above the figures set by a country, its central bank will lean toward a higher interest rate to cool inflationary pressures.

The expectation of a higher interest rate and the subsequent interest rate hike by the central bank will cause the currency to appreciate.

Key point: When CPI figures are higher than expected, the currency tends to strengthen in anticipation of an interest rate hike.

Purchasing Manufacturing Index

In the United States, the Purchasing Manufacturing Index (PMI) measures the activity level of about 400 purchasing managers in the manufacturing sector. A reading above 50 indicates expansion, and a reading below 50 indicates contraction.

Purchasing managers are surveyed on five subtopics with these breakdowns:

1. Production level—25%
2. New orders—30%
3. Supplier deliveries—15%
4. Inventories—10%
5. Employment level—20%

Traders watch these surveys closely because purchasing managers have early access to data about their company's performance. Hence the PMI alone can act as a leading indicator for the overall economic health of the country. A rising trend has a positive effect on the nation's currency.

Variations of the PMI include:

- Institute for Supply Management (ISM) *Non-Manufacturing Report on Business* (United States)
- Construction PMI (Great Britain)
- Services PMI (United States, Great Britain)
- Ivey PMI (Canada)

Key point: When PMI figures are higher than expected, the currency tends to strengthen.

Retail Sales

Figures for retail sales give the best gauge for consumer spending and possible clues into inflation data and, ultimately, the direction of interest rates. Retail sales track the dollar value of merchandise sold within the retail trade by sampling companies engaged in the business of selling end products to consumers. Generally, the most volatile components are transportation, accommodation, and food prices.

If retail sales growth is stagnant or slowing down, it tells us that consumers are not spending at previous levels, and could signal a recession due to the fact that personal consumption is needed to maintain robust growth in the economy.

Key point: When retail sales figures are higher than expected, the currency tends to strengthen in anticipation of an interest rate hike.

Rule of 20

News traders compare three different news figures:

1. Previous
2. Forecast
3. Actual

Previous figures denote the data that were last released. Forecast figures tell us what the analysts or economists expect the figures to be this time round. Actual figures are the reported data when they come out. Here's an inside scoop: *Traders trade based on expectations.* This means that the previous figures are not really important to their trading decisions. In fact, on their own, forecasted figures do not have much weight either.

The trick is to compare the forecasted figures with the actual figures. This is where the Rule of 20 comes in. The Rule of 20 states: *If the deviation between the actual and forecasted figures exceeds 20%, trade in the direction of the deviation.*

Let's use the U.S. NFP as an example. If forecasted figures are 300K, a 20% deviation is 60K. This means we can long the U.S. dollar if NFP numbers come in above 360K, or we can short the U.S. dollar if NFP numbers come in below 240K. Specifically, going long on the U.S. dollar means going long on USD/JPY or going short on EUR/USD. Similarly, going short on the U.S. dollar means going short on USD/JPY or going long on EUR/USD.

There are two special cases for the Rule of 20: *PMI and interest rates.* For PMI, the deviation between the actual and forecasted figures must exceed 50 basis points (0.5%) before a trade can be taken. For interest rates, the deviation between the actual and forecasted figures must exceed 20 basis points (0.2%) before a trade can be taken.

Let's look at how the Rule of 20 is applied to two strategies, gawk the talk and balk the talk.

STRATEGY 5: GAWK THE TALK

Time Frame

Gawk the talk works with the 15-minute (M15) or 30-minute (M30) candle. This means that each candle on the chart represents 15 minutes or 30 minutes of price movement.

Indicators

No indicators are used for this strategy.

Currency Pairs

The gawk the talk strategy is suitable for all currency pairs listed on the broker's platform, especially the seven major currency pairs of:

EUR/USD

USD/JPY

GBP/USD

USD/CHF

USD/CAD

AUD/USD

NZD/USD

Strategy Concept

We use either the M15 or M30 charts to determine our entries because the news is usually released in 15-minute intervals. Examples include 8 A.M., 9:15 A.M., 10:30 P.M., and 11:45 P.M.

As discussed in the Rule of 20, trades are taken by comparing the forecasted figures with the actual figures. For this strategy, we go long on the affected currency when actual figures are greater than forecasted figures by a minimum factor of 20%. Since we trade in currency pairs, we focus on pairs which feature the U.S. dollar in either the base currency or counter currency.

As an example, if the news is a positive interest rate announcement by the Reserve Bank of Australia, we will take a long trade on the AUD/USD. If the news is a positive retail sales announcement by Switzerland, we take a short trade on the USD/CHF.

What about news announcements by the United States?

For news that affects the United States directly, it is best for us to trade the two most liquid pairs: EUR/USD and USD/JPY.

In summary, if the affected currency is the base currency, we go long on the currency pair. If the affected currency is the counter currency, we go short.

Long Trade Setup

We use the Australian employment data on the M15 time frame for illustrating a long trade. Here are the steps to execute the gawk the talk strategy for long:

1. Identify the currency to trade the news (AUD employment change).
2. Enter long on AUD/USD once the actual figure released is higher than the forecasted figure by 20% or more. (See Figure 7.15.)
3. Set a stop loss of 20 pips from the entry price.
4. Set a profit target of 40 pips from the entry price. (See Figure 7.16.)

From the long example in Figure 7.17:

$$\text{Entry price} = 1.0303$$
$$\text{Stop loss} = 1.0283$$
$$\text{Profit target} = 1.0343$$

The risk for this trade is 20 pips, and the reward is 40 pips. The risk to reward ratio is 1:2, which yields a tidy 6% return if we take a 3% risk.

AUD Employment Change on 12 Apr 2012
Forecast: 6.4K, Actual: 44.0K

FIGURE 7.15 Enter Long on AUD/USD

FIGURE 7.16 Set Stop Loss and Profit Target

FIGURE 7.17 Trade Hits Profit Target

Short Trade Setup

We use the Swiss CPI to illustrate a short trade. Here are the steps to execute the gawk the talk strategy for short:

1. Identify the currency to trade for the news (CHF CPI month on month [m/m]).
2. Enter short on USD/CHF once the actual figure released is higher than the forecasted figure by 20% or more. (See Figure 7.18.)
3. Set a stop loss of 20 pips from the entry price.
4. Set a profit target of 40 pips from the entry price. (See Figure 7.19.)

From the short example in Figure 7.20:

$$\text{Entry price} = 0.9167$$
$$\text{Stop loss} = 0.9147$$
$$\text{Profit target} = 0.9107$$

The risk for this trade is 20 pips, and the reward is 40 pips. The risk to reward ratio is 1:2, which yields a tidy 6% return if we take a 3% risk.

Strategy Roundup

This strategy takes advantage of the market reaction when the actual figures for the affected currency are higher than the forecasted figures by a minimum factor of 20%.

FIGURE 7.18 Enter Short on USD/CHF

Source: Created with FX Primus Ltd, a PRIME Mantle Corporation PLC company. All rights reserved.

FIGURE 7.19 Set Stop Loss and Profit Target

FIGURE 7.20 Trade Hits Profit Target

1. For any news site you utilize, please remember to sync the timing of the news announcement to match the time zone of the country you are in.
2. Be mindful of whether the affected currency is in the base or counter currency of the forex quote. As an example, strong figures for USD would constitute a long trade on the USD/JPY but a short trade on the EUR/USD.

STRATEGY 6: BALK THE TALK

Fear is a greater driving force than pleasure. Humans tend to react more drastically in times of fear, or when they are presented with bad news. Fear is also the emotion that drives traders around the world to watch every single news announcement, for fear of missing out on key information.

Fear also results in sell-offs. Whenever there is bad news, the first reaction of traders is to sell. This is precisely why I mentioned in Chapter 5 that trading the news is one of the best ways I know of making good profits in a short time with bearable risk, especially since you can make a profit from either buying or selling.

Let's see how bad news can become profitable news for traders like you and me.

Time Frame

Balk the talk works with the 15-minute (M15) or 30-minute (M30) candle. This means that each candle on the chart represents 15 minutes or 30 minutes of price movement.

Indicators

No indicators are used for this strategy.

Currency Pairs

This strategy is suitable for all currency pairs listed on the broker's platform, especially the seven major currency pairs of:

EUR/USD
USD/JPY
GBP/USD
USD/CHF
USD/CAD
AUD/USD
NZD/USD

Strategy Concept

We use either the M15 or M30 charts to determine our entries because the news is usually released in 15-minute intervals. Examples include 8 A.M., 9:15 A.M., 10:30 P.M., and 11:45 P.M.

As discussed in the Rule of 20, trades are taken by comparing the forecasted figures with the actual figures. For this strategy, we go short on the affected currency when actual figures are lower than forecasted figures by a minimum factor of 20%.

Since we trade in currency pairs, we focus on pairs which feature the U.S. dollar in either the base currency or counter currency. As an example, if the news is a negative GDP announcement by Canada, we take a long trade on the USD/CAD.

If the news is a negative employment announcement by the United States, we take a long trade on EUR/USD or a short trade on USD/JPY.

Long Trade Setup

We use the Canadian gross domestic product (GDP) on M30 time frame for illustrating a long trade.

Here are the steps to execute the balk the talk strategy for long:

1. Identify the currency to trade the news (CAD GDP m/m).

2. Enter long on USD/CAD once the actual figure released is lower than the forecasted figure by 20% or more. (See Figure 7.21.)

3. Set a stop loss of 20 pips from the entry price.

4. Set a profit target of 40 pips from the entry price. (See Figure 7.22.)

CAD GDP m/m on 31 Jan 2012
Forecast: 0.2%, Actual: –0.1%

FIGURE 7.21   Enter Long on USD/CAD

Source: Created with FX Primus Ltd, a PRIME Mantle Corporation PLC company. All rights reserved.

FIGURE 7.22 Set Stop Loss and Profit Target

Source: Created with FX Primus Ltd, a PRIME Mantle Corporation PLC company. All rights reserved.

FIGURE 7.23 Trade Hits Profit Target

Source: Created with FX Primus Ltd, a PRIME Mantle Corporation PLC company. All rights reserved.

From the long example in Figure 7.23:

$$\text{Entry price} = 0.9983$$
$$\text{Stop loss} = 0.9963$$
$$\text{Profit target} = 1.0023$$

The risk for this trade is 20 pips, and the reward is 40 pips. The risk to reward ratio is 1:2, which yields a tidy 6% return if we take a 3% risk.

Short Trade Setup

We use the interest rate announcement by Reserve Bank of Australia on M30 time frame to illustrate a short trade. Here are the steps to execute the balk the talk strategy for short:

1. Identify the currency to trade the news (AUD interest rate).
2. Enter short on AUD/USD once the actual figure released is lower than the forecasted figure by 20 basis points (0.2%) or more. (See Figure 7.24.)
3. Set a stop loss of 20 pips from the entry price.
4. Set a profit target of 40 pips from the entry price. (See Figure 7.25.)

From the short example in Figure 7.26:

$$\text{Entry price} = 1.0410$$
$$\text{Stop loss} = 1.0430$$
$$\text{Profit target} = 1.0370$$

AUD Cash Rate on 1 May 2012
Forecast: 4%, Actual: 3.75%

FIGURE 7.24   Enter Short on AUD/USD

FIGURE 7.25 Set Stop Loss and Profit Target

Source: Created with FX Primus Ltd, a PRIME Mantle Corporation PLC company. All rights reserved.

FIGURE 7.26 Trade Hits Profit Target

The risk for this trade is 20 pips, and the reward is 40 pips. The risk to reward ratio is 1:2, which yields a tidy 6% return if we take a 3% risk.

Strategy Roundup

This strategy takes advantage of the market reaction when the actual figures for the affected currency are lower than the forecasted figures by a minimum factor of 20%.

Before taking a trade, it is important to note whether the affected currency is in the base currency or counter currency. As an example, if CHF is the affected currency, we look to go long on USD/CHF. If AUD is the affected currency, we look to go short on the AUD/USD.

Pay attention to the two special cases for Rule of 20: PMI and interest rates. For interest rates, the deviation has to be more than 20 basis points (0.2%). For PMI, the deviation has to be more than 50 basis points (0.5%).

CHAPTER 8

Strategies for Swing Traders

You are a swing trader primarily because you have a full-time job and don't have much time to analyze the markets. That is why your trading strategy is considered fairly midterm, with several trading opportunities in a week. Depending on the currency pair, the profit potential per trade for swing traders can range from 50 pips to 150 pips or more. With trades having profits as high as the daily volatility, it is normal for these trades to take more than a day to exit.

Most swing trading strategies use indicators to pinpoint entries. This chapter covers five strategies suitable for all swing traders. The techniques are developed for use on middle time frames, such as the hourly (H1) and the 4-hourly (H4) charts.

Due to the strategies' time frame, swing traders are presented with trading opportunities that most likely last more than a day but exit within a week.

STRATEGY 7: TREND RIDER

Two of the most popular quotes in the forex market are the sentences "The trend is your friend until it bends" and "Always trade along the trend." Each is good advice.

One of the main reasons why many retail traders fail to make consistent income is because they exit too early. How often have we had that experience when we jump into a trade, watch in delight as it goes our way, take a 30 pip profit with a smug grin, and then watch in horror as the trade goes another 500 pips in our direction?

The strategy discussed here will help traders of all levels, because it essentially prevents us from exiting our trade too early. This is achieved by not setting a predetermined profit target level but by employing a momentum indicator called the average directional movement index (ADX) to tell us when to exit the trade. I use this strategy often, because it only needs little monitoring but the payoff potential is huge.

Time Frame

The trend rider method works with the hourly (H1) or 4-hourly (H4) chart. This means that each candle on the chart represents 1 hour or 4 hours of price movement respectively.

Indicators

We use three indicators for this strategy:

1. Exponential moving average (EMA) with period 12 (EMA 12).
2. EMA with period 36 (EMA 36).
3. Average Directional Movement Index with Meta Trader 4 default setting (ADX 14). A level of 40 is added.

To understand the EMA, we first define the simple moving average (SMA).

Simple Moving Average   An SMA is calculated by adding the closing price of the candlestick over a given number of periods and dividing this total sum by the number of periods. For example, SMA 12 is the sum of closing prices for 12 candles divided by 12. The figures are dynamic, which means that old data are dropped as new data are added. This rolling figure causes the moving average to move along the time scale.

Exponential Moving Average   The EMA is similar to the SMA except that more weight is given to recent prices. The formula for an EMA is:

$$\text{Exponential Percentage} = 2/(\text{Time Period} + 1)$$

For EMA 12:

$$\text{Exponential Percentage} = 2/(12 + 1) = 15\%$$

This means that the most recent candle will be weighted 15% of the value of the EMA. For SMA 12, each candle has a uniform weight of only 8.3% (100/12).

The advantage of using an EMA over the SMA is its ability to pick up on price changes faster. I select EMA 12 because 12-hourly candles give me half a day's worth of price action. EMA 36 is 36 hourly candles, giving me one and a half days' worth of price action. Twelve 4-hourly candles give me two days' worth of price action, and 36 4-hourly candles give me 6 days' worth of price action on the 4-hourly chart.

The combination of EMA 12 and EMA 36 on either the hourly or 4-hourly time frame is important to give me a feel of the market over this time period.

Average Directional Movement Index   The ADX indicator is used to measure the strength of a trend. It is plotted as a line with values ranging from 0 to 100.

A low reading indicates a weak trend while a high reading depicts a strong trend. The ADX is non-directional, which means it registers trend strength in both uptrends and downtrends. I select the level 40 as a guide to tell me when momentum of the trend is losing steam. The default setting is period 14, and this is the same setting we will use for the trend rider strategy.

Currency Pairs

The strategy is suitable for all currency pairs listed on the broker's platform, especially the seven major currency pairs of:

EUR/USD

USD/JPY

GBP/USD

USD/CHF

USD/CAD

AUD/USD

NZD/USD

Strategy Concept

The strategy uses moving average cross-over to detect an early change in momentum. Specifically, we get a signal to go long when the EMA 12 crosses above the EMA 36. Similarly, we get a signal to go short when the EMA 12 crosses below the EMA 36. The ADX indicator helps us to gauge the strength of the momentum. We set the 40 level as a benchmark, as any value above 40 indicates that momentum is very strong. Once the ADX crosses above 40 and comes back below, it is telling us that the momentum is losing steam and it's time to exit the trade. (See Figure 8.1.)

FIGURE 8.1 Trend Rider Strategy Concept

Long Trade Setup

I use the EUR/USD on the H4 time frame to illustrate a long trade. Here are the steps to execute the trend rider strategy for long:

1. Wait for the EMA 12 to cross above the EMA 36. (See Figure 8.2.)
2. Take an entry when the price comes back down to touch the EMA 12. (See Figure 8.3.)

FIGURE 8.2 EMA 12 Crosses EMA 36

FIGURE 8.3   Candlestick Touches EMA 12
Source: Created with FX Primus Ltd, a PRIME Mantle Corporation PLC company. All rights reserved.

FIGURE 8.4   Set Stop Loss and Profit Target
Source: Created with FX Primus Ltd, a PRIME Mantle Corporation PLC company. All rights reserved.

3. Set the stop loss at the EMA 36; note that it must be at least 30 pips from the entry price. There is no predetermined level for the profit target. (See Figure 8.4.)
4. Exit the trade when the ADX 14 crosses above 40 and drops back below. (See Figure 8.5.)

FIGURE 8.5 Exit Trade When ADX 14 Crosses Above 40 and Drops Back Below

From the long example in Figure 8.5:

$$\text{Entry price} = 1.2886$$
$$\text{Stop loss} = 1.2828$$
$$\text{Profit target} = 1.3202$$

The risk for this trade is 58 pips, and the reward is 316 pips. The risk to reward ratio is 1:5.4, which yields a whopping 16.2% return if we take a 3% risk.

Short Trade Setup

I use the AUD/USD on the H1 time frame to illustrate a short trade. Here are the steps to execute the trend rider strategy for short:

1. Wait for the EMA 12 to cross below the EMA 36. (See Figure 8.6.)
2. Take an entry when the price goes back up to touch the EMA 12. (See Figure 8.7.)
3. Set the stop loss at the EMA 36; note that it must be at least 30 pips from the entry price. There is no predetermined level for the profit target. (See Figure 8.8.)
4. Exit the trade when the ADX 14 crosses above 40 and drops back below. (See Figure 8.9.)

FIGURE 8.6   EMA 12 Crosses Below EMA 36

Source:

FIGURE 8.7   Candlestick Touches EMA 12

Source:

From the short example in Figure 8.9:

$$Entry\ price = 1.0505$$
$$Stop\ loss = 1.0543$$
$$Profit\ target = 1.0350$$

FIGURE 8.8 Set Stop Loss and Profit Target

Source: Created with FX Primus Ltd, a PRIME Mantle Corporation PLC company. All rights reserved.

FIGURE 8.9 Exit Trade When ADX 14 Crosses Above 40 and Drops Back Below

Source: Created with FX Primus Ltd, a PRIME Mantle Corporation PLC company. All rights reserved.

The risk for this trade is 38 pips, and the reward is 155 pips. The risk to reward ratio is 1:4, which yields a decent 12% return if we take a 3% risk.

Strategy Roundup

The trend rider is one of the most effective strategies in the swing traders' toolbox because there is no predetermined profit target.

One of the biggest reasons why retail traders fail to make good money in the forex market is because they exit too early, especially when the ongoing trade is registering a small profit. The use of the ADX indicator in this strategy prevents us from exiting a trade prematurely. Instead, it keeps us with the trend for the long haul. This is how big profits are generated.

Trend following is statistically valid in the sense that every successful trader vouches for it. Additionally, because of the highly favorable risk to reward ratio of trend following strategies, one good trade can more than compensate for the losses incurred during a bad patch. Again, the key to successful trend trading is not to cut your profits short.

STRATEGY 8: TREND BOUNCER

The trigger of a trend can be anything from a political decision, to a central bank policy announcement, to the discovery of new resources, to a myriad of other possibilities. Trends move like waves in that they ebb and flow.

In an uptrend, you will find that, at a certain point in time, prices will pull back or retrace before continuing with the upward movement. Similarly for a downtrend, prices will retrace upward against the downward momentum before continuing their way down again.

This ebb-and-flow movement frustrates many trend traders, because these retracements often stop out their trades while the market moves in their direction again later.

Experienced trend traders usually wait for the retracement to happen before taking a trade in the direction of the trend. This is how the trend bouncer strategy came about. The Bollinger Bands indicator provides an objective way of identifying the ebb-and-flow movement of a trend.

Since this is a trend strategy, we have more than one profit target. In fact, we have three specific profit levels for this strategy. The strategy differs slightly from the trend rider in that there are specific levels for trend bouncer traders to exit with profits.

Time Frame

The trend bouncer method works with the hourly (H1) or 4-hourly (H4) chart. This means that each candle on the chart represents 1 hour or 4 hours of price movement respectively.

Indicators

We use these indicators for this strategy:

1. Bollinger Bands (moving average [MA] 12, deviation [Dev] 2)
2. Bollinger Bands (MA 12, Dev 4)

Bollinger Band

Refer to the piranha strategy in Chapter 5 for an explanation on the Bollinger Bands indicator.

Currency Pairs

This strategy is suitable for all currency pairs listed on the broker's platform, especially the seven major currency pairs of:

EUR/USD

USD/JPY

GBP/USD

USD/CHF

USD/CAD

AUD/USD

NZD/USD

Strategy Concept

With the help of the Bollinger Bands, we can objectively identify the ebb-and-flow movement of a trend. When the candlestick hits the upper band of Bollinger Bands (MA 12, Dev 2), it indicates an upward momentum, and we prepare to go long. As prices retrace back to the MA 12 (the center line of the Bollinger Bands), a significant retracement has occurred, and it is a good time to enter for a long trade.

When the candlestick hits the lower band of the Bollinger Bands (MA 12, Dev 2), it indicates a downward momentum, and we prepare to go short. As prices retrace back to the MA12 (the center line of the Bollinger Bands), a significant retracement has occurred, and it is a good time to enter for a short trade. This trend strategy exits at three different targets.

Long Trade Setup

We use the GBP/USD on the H4 time frame to illustrate a long trade. Here are the steps to execute the trend bouncer strategy for long:

1. Wait for the price to hit the upper band of the first Bollinger Bands (MA 12, Dev 2) and retrace back down to the center MA 12. (See Figure 8.10.)

2. When the price touches MA 12, enter for a long. (See Figure 8.11.)

3. The stop loss is the lower band of the second Bollinger Bands (MA 12, Dev 4). (See Figure 8.12.)

4. The trade will have three profit targets with risk to reward ratios of 1:1, 1:2, and 1:3 respectively. (See Figure 8.13.)

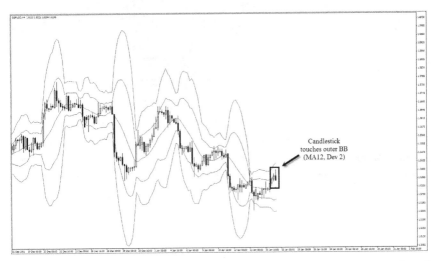

Candlestick touches outer BB (MA12, Dev 2)

FIGURE 8.10 Price Hits Upper Band of First Bollinger Bands (MA 12, Dev 2) and Retraces Down to the Center MA 12

Source: Created with FX Primus Ltd, a PRIME Mantle Corporation PLC company. All rights reserved.

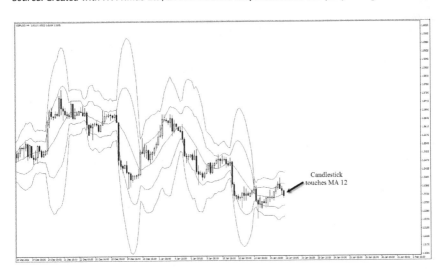

Candlestick touches MA 12

FIGURE 8.11 Price Touches MA 12

Source: Created with FX Primus Ltd, a PRIME Mantle Corporation PLC company. All rights reserved.

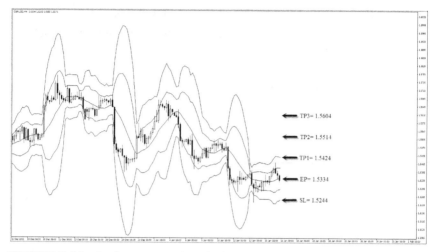

FIGURE 8.12 Set Stop Loss and Profit Targets

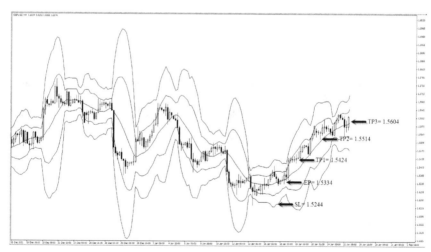

FIGURE 8.13 Trade Hits Profit Targets

From the long example in Figure 8.13:

$$Entry\ price = 1.5334$$
$$Stop\ loss = 1.5244$$
$$Profit\ target\ 1 = 1.5424$$
$$Profit\ target\ 2 = 1.5514$$
$$Profit\ target\ 3 = 1.5604$$

The risk for this trade is 90 pips, and the reward is 270 pips if all three targets are hit. The risk to reward ratio is 1:3, which yields a tidy 9% return if we take a 3% risk.

Short Trade Setup

We use the NZD/USD on H1 time frame to illustrate a short trade. Here are the steps to execute the trend bouncer strategy for short:

1. Wait for the price to hit the lower band of the first Bollinger Bands (MA 12, Dev 2) and retrace back up to the center MA 12. (See Figure 8.14.)
2. When the price touches MA 12, go for a short. (See Figure 8.15.)
3. The stop loss is the upper band of the second Bollinger Bands (MA 12, Dev 4). (See Figure 8.16.)
4. The trade will have three profit targets with risk to reward ratios of 1:1, 1:2, and 1:3 respectively. (See Figure 8.17.)

From the short example in Figure 8.17:

$$\text{Entry price} = 0.8214$$
$$\text{Stop loss} = 0.8260$$
$$\text{Profit target 1} = 0.8168$$
$$\text{Profit target 2} = 0.8122$$
$$\text{Profit target 3} = 0.8076$$

FIGURE 8.14 Price Hits Lower Band of First Bollinger Bands (MA 12, Dev 2) and Retraces Back Up to Center MA 12

Source: Created with FX Primus Ltd, a PRIME Mantle Corporation PLC company. All rights reserved.

FIGURE 8.15   Price Touches MA 12

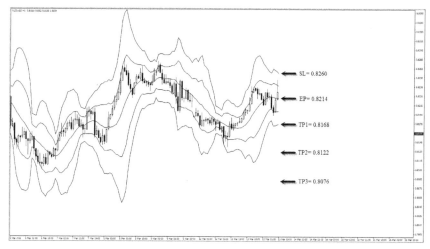

FIGURE 8.16   Set Stop Loss and Profit Targets

The risk for this trade is 46 pips, and the reward is 138 pips if all three targets are hit. The risk to reward ratio is 1:3, which yields a tidy 9% return if we take a 3% risk.

FIGURE 8.17 Trade Hits Profit Targets

Strategy Roundup

Understanding how trends move in ebbs and flows allow traders like you and me to identify the direction and timing of our entries. We enter during the "ebb" and let the "flow" ride us to our profit targets.

Unlike the trend rider strategy, the trend bouncer strategy has three predetermined profit targets. Traders who like to bank in profits in various stages prefer this strategy. The strategy is rooted in trend trading. With a momentum indicator like the Bollinger Bands, you will greatly increase your odds at being profitable in the long run.

Remember that smart money typically follows the trend. This strategy helps us to hop on board early when we identify the trend.

STRATEGY 9: FIFTH ELEMENT

"I am using a wonderful strategy, but I have to constantly monitor the market in order not to miss a trade." "Ah! I missed a trade again." "According to my strategy, it looks like there may be a trade setup soon, but I have a movie date in the next hour. What should I do?"

Do these scenarios sound familiar to you?

Wouldn't it be nice to have a strategy that actually prompts you when momentum of the market has switched to a new trend? In fact, the beauty of the fifth element strategy is that it tells you ahead of time when the entry price will be.

This is the third and final trend strategy in this segment. Let's find out what's so special about it.

Time Frame

The fifth element strategy works with the hourly (H1) or 4-hourly (H4) chart. This means that each candle on the chart represents 1 hour or 4 hours of price movement respectively.

Indicators

We use this indicator for this strategy:

Moving average convergence divergence (MACD) with default settings:
a. Fast EMA: 12
b. Slow EMA: 26
c. MACD SMA: 9
d. Apply to close.

The moving average was created by Gerald Appel in 1979. Today the MACD is one of the most popular indicators used by forex traders world-wide. The indicator calculates and displays the difference between the two EMAs at any time.

Since we are using the default setting, this difference is based on the EMA 12 and the EMA 26. As the market moves, the two moving averages move in tandem, widening (diverging) when the market is trending and tightening (converging) when the market is slowing down.

There are three important elements of the MACD indicator:

1. **MACD line.** This is the difference between the EMA 12 and the EMA 26.
2. **Signal.** This is the 9-day SMA of the MACD line.
3. **Histogram.** This is the difference between the MACD line and the signal.

It is important to recognize that the histogram is a derivative of the price and not the price itself. The histogram is positive when the MACD line is above its SMA 9 and negative when the MACD line is below its SMA 9.

When prices rise, the histogram bar becomes longer as the speed of the price movement accelerates; the bar contracts as price movement decelerates. The same principle applies when prices are falling, but the histogram bars form at the bottom.

Up until now, I have described the traditional MACD. In the fifth element strategy, we use the Meta Trader 4 MACD. The difference between the traditional MACD and the Meta Trader 4 MACD is in the histogram. The traditional MACD's histogram represents the difference between the MACD line and signal. The Meta Trader 4 MACD's histogram however, represents only the MACD line, which is the difference between the EMA 12 and EMA 26.

The histogram is important to help us identify possible shifts in momentum and acts as a confirmation of the momentum. This is the main essence of the fifth element.

Currency Pairs

This strategy is suitable for all currency pairs listed on the broker's platform, especially the seven major currency pairs of:

EUR/USD

USD/JPY

GBP/USD

USD/CHF

USD/CAD

AUD/USD

NZD/USD

Strategy Concept

The MACD histogram indicates the direction and momentum of the market. When the MACD histogram switches from negative to positive, this indicates a possible upward shift in momentum. We wait for five positive bars on the histogram to confirm the momentum before entering a long trade on the fifth bar. No prizes for guessing why the name of this strategy is called the fifth element!

When the MACD histogram switches from positive to negative, this indicates a possible downward shift in momentum. We wait for five negative bars of the histogram to confirm the momentum before entering a short trade on the fifth bar.

Long Trade Setup

We use the AUD/USD on the H4 time frame to illustrate a long trade. Here are the steps to execute the fifth element strategy for long:

1. Wait for the MACD histogram to go from negative (<0) to positive (>0). (See Figure 8.18.)
2. Wait for four positive bars to form on the histogram before going long on the opening candle of the fifth histogram. (See Figure 8.19.)
3. Set the stop loss at the last low of the histogram.
4. The trade will have two profit targets with risk to reward ratios of 1:1 and 1:2 respectively. (See Figure 8.20.)

From the long example in Figure 8.21:

$$\text{Entry price} = 1.0300$$
$$\text{Stop loss} = 1.0150$$
$$\text{Profit target 1} = 1.0450$$
$$\text{Profit target 2} = 1.0600$$

The risk for this trade is 150 pips, and the reward is 300 pips if both targets are hit. The risk to reward ratio is 1:2, which yields a tidy 6% return if we take a 3% risk.

FIGURE 8.18   MACD Histogram Goes from Negative to Positive

Source: Created with FX Primus Ltd, a PRIME Mantle Corporation PLC company. All rights reserved.

FIGURE 8.19   Four Positive Bars Form Before Going Long

FIGURE 8.20   Set Stop Loss and Profit Targets

Short Trade Setup

We use the EUR/USD on the H4 time frame to illustrate a short trade. Here are the steps to execute the fifth element strategy for short:

1. Wait for the MACD histogram to go from positive (<0) to negative (>0). (See Figure 8.22.)

FIGURE 8.21 Trade Hits Profit Targets

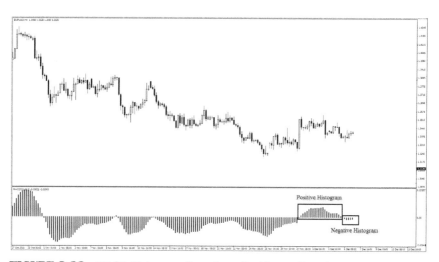

FIGURE 8.22 MACD Histogram Goes from Positive to Negative

2. Wait for four negative bars of the histogram before going short on the opening candle of the fifth histogram. (See Figure 8.23.)

3. Set the stop loss at the last high of the histogram.

4. The trade will have two profit targets with risk to reward ratios of 1:1 and 1:2 respectively. (See Figure 8.24.)

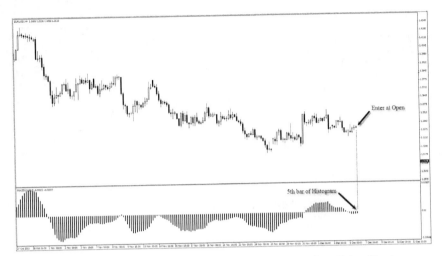

FIGURE 8.23 Four Negative Bars Form on Histogram Before Going Short

FIGURE 8.24 Set Stop Loss and Profit Targets

From the short example in Figure 8.25:

$$\text{Entry price} = 1.3400$$
$$\text{Stop loss} = 1.3547$$
$$\text{Profit target 1} = 1.3253$$
$$\text{Profit target 2} = 1.3106$$

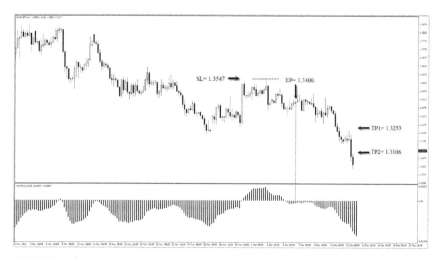

FIGURE 8.25   Trade Hits Profit Targets

The risk for this trade is 147 pips, and the reward is 294 pips if both targets are hit. The risk to reward ratio is 1:2, which yields a tidy 6% return if we take a 3% risk.

Strategy Roundup

The fifth element is an excellent swing trading strategy for beginners. The beauty of this strategy is that it does not require you to monitor the market for a long time. It also signals you well in advance as to when the entry of a trade is about to take place. As you know by now, the entry takes place on the fifth bar after the MACD histogram switches from negative to positive or from positive to negative.

Five bars of the histogram is equivalent to 5 hours on the H1 time frame or 20 hours on the H4 time frame. This means you need to monitor the market only on a 5-hourly basis if you are trading the H1 time frame or a 20-hourly basis if you are trading the H4 time frame. Knowing that the entry is always on the fifth bar of the histogram means that you are in total control of your time.

As an example, let's say that you are trading the H1 time frame. You spot the MACD histogram switching from negative to positive. You glance at your watch and see that the time is 2:15 P.M.

The current bar is the first bar, and it corresponds to the 2 P.M. candle. What would be the likely time that you will enter the trade? The answer is

6 P.M., because that would be the start of the candle that corresponds to the fifth bar of the histogram. You have ample time to catch a two-hour movie before heading home again to prepare for the trade!

STRATEGY 10: POWER RANGER

The forex market either trends or ranges. The last three strategies were dedicated to trading the trend. The next two strategies are used to trade the range.

Range strategies are based either on pure price action or on indicators, or using a combination of both. Oscillators are a class of indicators that are commonly used in range strategies, because the oscillator indicates a possible range that the price swings back and forth from.

Some common oscillators are the stochastic and the relative strength index (RSI). As a trader and coach, I have found that identifying ranges poses more challenges to traders than identifying trends. After all, a range looks obvious to us only after it is formed.

To make matters worse, when a range is clearly formed and we are using a range strategy, price action soars and causes the market to break out of a range again. Hence, identifying the range while it is still forming offers a huge advantage to traders.

The power ranger strategy serves to fill this gap. Let us take a look at how this is done through the use of a powerful oscillator.

Time Frame

The power ranger method works with the hourly (H1) or 4-hourly (H4) chart. This means that each candle on the chart represents 1 hour or 4 hours of price movement respectively.

Indicators

We use the stochastic indicator for this strategy with these settings:

%K period = 10

%D period = 3

Slowing = 3

Price field = High/Low

MA method = Simple

Levels 20 and 80

Formula

$$\%K = 100[(C - L10) / (H10 - L10)]$$

Where:

C = most recent closing price

L10 = low of the last 10 periods

H10 = high of the last 10 periods

%D = 3-period moving average of %K

Stochastic Indicator   Stochastic is an oscillator that measures overbought and oversold conditions in the market.

How to Apply Stochastic   Stochastic tells us when the market is overbought or oversold. When the stochastic lines are above 80, the market is overbought. When the stochastic lines are below 20, the market is oversold. As a general rule of thumb, oversold gives us a buy signal, and overbought gives us a sell signal.

Looking at the chart in Figure 8.26, you can see that the stochastic has been showing overbought and oversold conditions respectively. Based on this information, because the market was overbought for such a long period of time, we expect the price to go down soon.

FIGURE 8.26   Illustration of Stochastic Indicator

Source: Created with FX Primus Ltd, a PRIME Mantle Corporation PLC company. All rights reserved.

That is the basics of the stochastic. Many traders use the stochastic in different ways, but the main purpose of the indicator is to show us where the market is overbought and oversold.

Currency Pairs

This strategy is suitable for all currency pairs listed on the broker's platform, especially the seven major currency pairs of:

EUR/USD

USD/JPY

GBP/USD

USD/CHF

USD/CAD

AUD/USD

NZD/USD

Strategy Concept

The power ranger strategy is based on the concept that a range will form after the market finishes trending. We use the stochastic to give us an indication of a possible range formation. We also rely on the current market momentum to tell us when to go long or short. If the market is moving in an uptrend, we look to go long in the range. The entry is determined by the oversold region (below level 20) of the stochastic.

If the market is moving in a downtrend, we look to go short in the range. The entry is determined by the overbought region (above level 80) of the stochastic. We use the most recent high and low to determine the possible resistance and support of the range.

This strategy has two profit targets, and we take the first profit target within the range. The second profit target is located beyond the range in anticipation of a breakout opportunity.

Long Trade Setup

We use EUR/USD on the H1 time frame to illustrate a long trade. Here are the steps to execute the power ranger strategy for long:

1. Draw an uptrend line based on a series of higher highs and higher lows. (See Figure 8.27.)
2. On the stochastic, look for %K and %D to go below level 20 (oversold). (See Figure 8.28.)

FIGURE 8.27　Draw Uptrend Line Based on Series of Higher Highs and Higher Lows

Source: Created with FX Primus Ltd, a PRIME Mantle Corporation PLC company. All rights reserved.

FIGURE 8.28　On the Stochastic, Look for %K and %D to Go Above Level 20 (Oversold)

Source: Created with FX Primus Ltd, a PRIME Mantle Corporation PLC company. All rights reserved.

3. Determine the support and resistance of the range. Enter long once the stochastic crosses above level 20.

4. Set the first profit target at the 75% mark of the range. Set the stop loss at a risk to reward ratio of 1:1, and set the second profit target at risk to reward ratio of 1:2. After calculation, the stop loss must be below the support level. If not, the trade is considered invalid. (See Figure 8.29.)

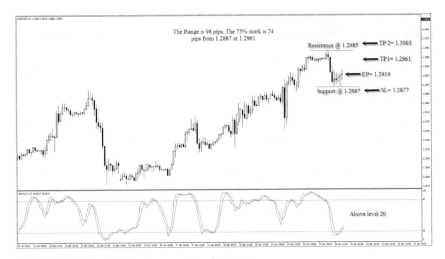

FIGURE 8.29 Set Stop Loss and Profit Targets

Source: Created with FX Primus Ltd, a PRIME Mantle Corporation PLC company. All rights reserved.

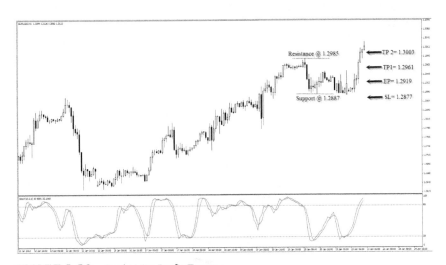

FIGURE 8.30 Trade Hits Profit Targets

Source: Created with FX Primus Ltd, a PRIME Mantle Corporation PLC company. All rights reserved.

From the long example in Figure 8.30:

Entry price = 1.2919
Stop loss = 1.2877
Profit target 1 = 1.2961
Profit target 2 = 1.3003

The risk for this trade is 42 pips, and the reward is 84 pips if both targets are hit. The risk to reward ratio is 1:2, which yields a tidy 6% return if we take a 3% risk.

Short Trade Setup

We use AUD/USD on the H1 time frame to illustrate a short trade. Here are the steps to execute the power ranger strategy for short:

1. Draw a downtrend line based on a series of lower highs and lower lows. (See Figure 8.31.)
2. On the stochastic, look for %K and %D to go above level 80 (oversold). (See Figure 8.32.)
3. Determine the support and resistance of the range. Enter short once the stochastic goes below level 80.
4. Set the first profit target at the 75% mark of the range. Set the stop loss at a risk to reward ratio of 1:1, and set the second profit target at risk to reward ratio of 1:2. After calculation, the stop loss must be above the resistance level. If not, the trade is considered invalid. (See Figure 8.33.)

FIGURE 8.31   Draw a Downtrend Line Based on a Series of Lower Highs and Lower Lows

Source: Created with FX Primus Ltd, a PRIME Mantle Corporation PLC company. All rights reserved.

FIGURE 8.32 On the Stochastic, Look for %K and %D to Go Below Level 80 (Oversold)

Source: Created with FX Primus Ltd, a PRIME Mantle Corporation PLC company. All rights reserved.

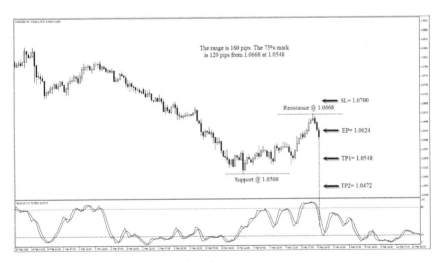

FIGURE 8.33 Set Stop Loss and Profit Targets

Source: Created with FX Primus Ltd, a PRIME Mantle Corporation PLC company. All rights reserved.

From the short example in Figure 8.34:

$$\text{Entry price} = 1.0624$$
$$\text{Stop loss} = 1.0700$$
$$\text{Profit target 1} = 1.0548$$
$$\text{Profit target 2} = 1.0472$$

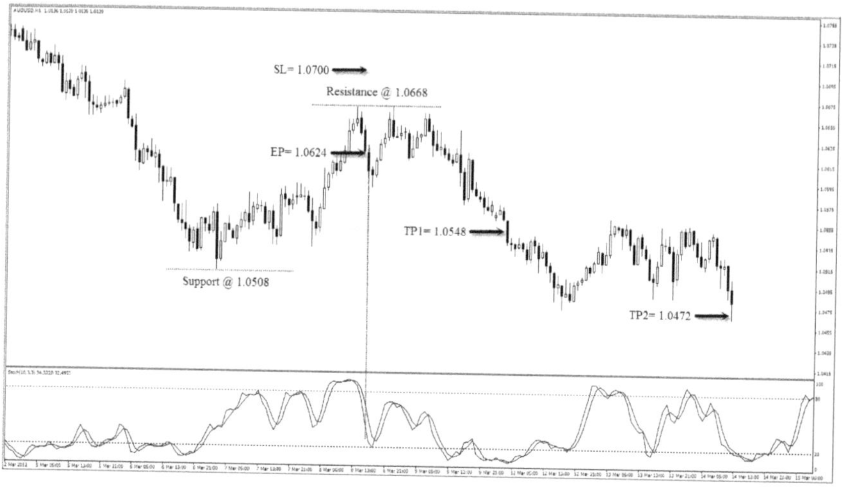

FIGURE 8.34 Trade Hits Profit Targets

Source: Created with FX Primus Ltd, a PRIME Mantle Corporation PLC company.

The risk for this trade is 76 pips, and the reward is 152 pips if both targets are hit. The risk to reward ratio is 1:2, which yields a tidy 6% return if we take a 3% risk.

Strategy Roundup

This is an awesome range strategy as it allows us to take a range trade in the early stages of formation. The bonus is that it also allows us to take advantage of a second profit target in the event prices break out of a range and move into an early trend.

It doesn't mean that you should go long whenever the stochastic is at the oversold region or go short whenever the stochastic is at the overbought region. If you do so, you may end up selling on an uptrend or buying on a downtrend. Going against momentum in this way can be risky.

Always determine the momentum of the market *first* before deciding whether to look for the overbought or oversold region of the stochastic. In an uptrend, look for the oversold region. In a downtrend, look for the overbought region. In this way, you will be trading along with the market momentum and putting yourself in an advantageous position.

Determining the momentum of the market *first* prevents us from blindly trading the signal given by the stochastic.

STRATEGY 11: THE PENDULUM

In the previous strategy, we explored a technique that helps us to anticipate a range with the help of the stochastic indicator and also trade it in the early stages of formation. The pendulum strategy comes to the rescue in the later stages of a range formation. In other words, we can still trade the range after it has been formed.

You don't need any indicators for this strategy, and you can use it to trade a range for as long as the market is swinging back and forth within the range like a pendulum.

Time Frame

The pendulum method works with the hourly (H1) or 4-hourly (H4) chart. This means that each candle on the chart represents 1 hour or 4 hours of price movement respectively.

Indicators

No indicators are used for this strategy.

Currency Pairs

This strategy is suitable for all currency pairs listed on the broker's platform, especially the seven major currency pairs of:

EUR/USD

USD/JPY

GBP/USD

USD/CHF

USD/CAD

AUD/USD

NZD/USD

Strategy Concept

The pendulum in motion swings back and forth because the force of gravity is pulling it back to the vertical position every time it swings away from it. The pendulum reaches an optimal height before it starts to fall back. However, if the swinging force is too great, the string holding the pendulum will snap, and the pendulum will fly off.

The ranging market acts in a similar fashion to the pendulum. Every time prices pull away from the midpoint of the range toward the support or resistance, market forces will pull it back towards the mid-point of the range. However, when the market gathers enough momentum, prices will break the support or resistance of the range and move into a trend.

In this strategy, we wait for the pendulum to reach its optimal height and fall before we enter the trade. We do this by executing a trade only at the 10% mark after prices turn back from either support or resistance. The first target is set at the 50% mark of the range, and the second target is set at the 90% mark of the range.

Long Trade Setup

We use the AUD/USD on the H4 time frame to illustrate a long trade. Here are the steps to execute the pendulum strategy for long:

1. Identify the resistance and support. Take note when the price goes back to the support again. (See Figure 8.35.)
2. In this example, the range is 269 pips; 10% of the range is 27 pips. Enter when the price bounces 27 pips above the support (1.0101). (See Figure 8.36.)
3. The first and second profit targets are 50% and 90% of the range respectively, which are 135 pips and 243 pips above the support (1.0101).
4. Use risk to reward ratio of 1:1 to set the stop loss. (See Figure 8.37.)

FIGURE 8.35   Identify Resistance and Support

Source: Created with FX Primus Ltd, a PRIME Mantle Corporation PLC company. All rights reserved.

FIGURE 8.36   Enter When Price Bounces 27 Pips Above Support

FIGURE 8.37   Set Stop Loss and Profit Targets

From the long example in Figure 8.38:

$$\text{Entry price} = 1.0128$$
$$\text{Stop loss} = 1.0020$$
$$\text{Profit target 1} = 1.0236$$
$$\text{Profit target 2} = 1.0344$$

FIGURE 8.38 Trade Hits Profit Target

The risk for this trade is 108 pips, and the reward is 216 pips if both targets are hit. The risk to reward ratio is 1:2, which yields a tidy 6% return if we take a 3% risk.

Short Trade Setup

We use the GBP/USD on the H4 time frame to illustrate a short trade. Here are the steps to execute the pendulum strategy for short:

1. Identify the resistance and support. Take note when price goes back to the resistance again. (See Figure 8.39.)
2. In this example, the range is 205 pips; 10% of the range is 21 pips. Enter when the price bounces 21 pips below the resistance (1.6117). (See Figure 8.40.)
3. The first and second profit targets are 50% and 90% of the range respectively, which are 103 pips and 185 pips below the resistance (1.6117).
4. Use risk to reward ratio of 1:1 to set the stop loss. (See Figure 8.41.)

From the long example in Figure 8.42:

$$Entry\ price = 1.6096$$
$$Stop\ loss = 1.6178$$
$$Profit\ target\ 1 = 1.6014$$
$$Profit\ target\ 2 = 1.5932$$

FIGURE 8.39   Identify Resistance and Support

FIGURE 8.40   Enter When Price Bounces 21 Pips Below Resistance

The risk for this trade is 82 pips, and the reward is 164 pips if both targets are hit. The risk to reward ratio is 1:2, which yields a tidy 6% return if we take a 3% risk.

FIGURE 8.41   Set Stop Loss and Profit Targets

Source: Created with FX Primus Ltd, a PRIME Mantle Corporation PLC company. All rights reserved.

FIGURE 8.42   Trade Hits Profit Targets

Source: Created with FX Primus Ltd, a PRIME Mantle Corporation PLC company. All rights reserved.

Strategy Roundup

This strategy is applicable as long as the market is swinging back and forth in a range. The power ranger strategy and the pendulum strategy work perfectly together. You can use the power ranger strategy to identify and trade the range in its early stage of formation, then apply the pendulum strategy to trade the later portion of the range.

CHAPTER 9

Strategies for Position Traders

Three characteristics define you as a position trader:

1. You have a deep understanding of market fundamentals.

2. You are not concerned with the short-term and medium-term movements of the currency market.

3. You have a sizable account to trade with. This is necessary to support your long-term outlook and withstand possible large floating losses should the trade go against you for an extended period of time.

Two advantages come into play for position traders. The first point is that interest can be earned. This is because interest or swap is paid on the currency that is borrowed and earned on the one that is bought. This amount can be significant when trades are held for long periods of time.

Secondly, correlations between other financial instruments can be brought into play. In the financial world, capital flows in a fairly predictable manner. Position traders who have a great feel for the market can use their knowledge to predict how other markets will correlate to the flow of money in the forex market.

A great example is the commodity market. When risk is on, commodity currencies, such as the Australian dollar, the New Zealand dollar, and the Canadian dollar, tend to do well. Over time, the strengthening of these 3 currencies also translate into higher prices for the actual commodities involved. Examples include gold and oil.

This chapter explores three strategies with time frames of either the daily or weekly charts. The two aspects of position trading—swap and commodity correlation—are also explored to allow position traders to achieve maximum gains across several asset classes.

STRATEGY 12: SWAP AND FLY

Every forex transaction involves the borrowing of one currency to buy another. This transaction also forms the basis of why traders can go long or short at any time.

As an example, if you are buying a currency with a higher interest rate than the one you are borrowing, the net interest rate differential will be positive, and you earn interest for every day that the trade remains open. Conversely, if the interest rate differential is negative, you will have to pay interest for every day that the trade remains open. You may know this as the carry trade.

Five P.M. in New York is considered the beginning and end of the forex trading day. Hence, any trading positions that are open beyond 5 P.M. are considered to be held overnight—or rolled over—and are subject to swap rates. The forex market is closed on Saturdays and Sundays, so no swap rate is incurred or earned over the weekend. However, most liquidity providers still apply the swap rules over the weekend.

To balance the effect of non-trading activities over the weekend, the forex market books three days of swap on Wednesday. Hence, if you hold a trade over 5 P.M. on a Wednesday evening, you will either incur or earn three times the normal rates.

The swap and fly strategy is a slow but steady technique that helps you to accumulate interest every day. You can even come out with a positive return after a period of time, even though the trade exits at breakeven.

Figures 9.1 and 9.2 show how you can track which currency pairs give positive swap when you execute a long or short position in the currency market. Do note, however, that figures may be different for different brokers.

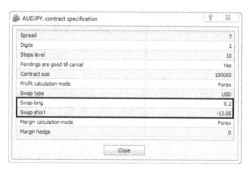

FIGURE 9.1   Positive Swap for Long Trades on AUD/JPY

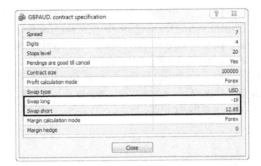

GBPAUD. contract specification	
Spread	7
Digits	4
Stops level	20
Pendings are good till cancel	Yes
Contract size	100000
Profit calculation mode	Forex
Swap type	USD
Swap long	-19
Swap short	12.85
Margin calculation mode	Forex
Margin hedge	0

Close

FIGURE 9.2 Positive Swap for Short Trades on GBP/AUD

Time Frame

The swap and fly method works with the daily candle (D1) and weekly candle (W1). This means that each candle on the chart represents 1 day or 1 week of price movement.

Indicators

No indicators are used for this strategy.

Currency Pairs

This strategy is suitable for all currency pairs listed on the broker's platform that have positive swaps for either long or short positions.

Strategy Concept

The main aim of this strategy is to earn as much interest as we can. Hence the first step is to find out which currency pairs on the broker's platform offer the highest swap rates for both long and short positions.

If a positive swap is given on a long position, we look for a suitable long entry on the chart. If a positive swap is given on a short position, we look for a suitable short entry on the chart.

The next milestone is to shift the stop loss dynamically to the entry price, also known as the break-even price. This step is done when the market moves favorably in our direction. After a period of time, even if our "new" stop-loss level is hit, the trade is exited with a profit because of the swap earned.

This strategy can be used in conjunction with any other high-time frame strategies. To illustrate the effect of this strategy, I am going to use common candlestick patterns, such as three white soldiers and three black crows, to illustrate a long and a short trade.

Three white soldiers is a bullish candlestick pattern consisting of three consecutive bull candles. Three black crows is a bearish candlestick pattern consisting of three consecutive bear candles.

Long Trade Setup

We use the AUD/JPY on the daily time frame to illustrate the long setup. Here are the steps to execute the swap and fly strategy for long:

1. Identify a three white soldiers candlestick pattern. (See Figure 9.3.)
2. Enter long at the opening of the next candle.
3. Reference a recent significant low to set the stop loss. (See Figure 9.4.)
4. Once the market moves in your favor at a risk to reward ratio of 1:1, shift your stop loss to the entry price. (See Figure 9.5.)
5. Trade hits breakeven after 36 weeks (252 days). (See Figure 9.6.)

FIGURE 9.3   Identify a Three White Soldiers Candlestick Pattern
Source: Created with FX Primus Ltd, a PRIME Mantle Corporation PLC company. All rights reserved.

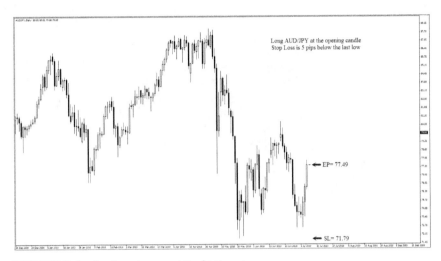

FIGURE 9.4 Set Stop Loss and Profit Target

FIGURE 9.5 Stop Loss Shifted to Entry Price

From the long example in Figure 9.6:

The swap for holding a long AUD/JPY position was AUD12 for every standard lot. This is equivalent to 1.2 pips. The swap per week is 1.2 pips × 7 = 8.4 pips. The swap for 36 weeks is 8.4 pips × 36 = 302.4 pips.

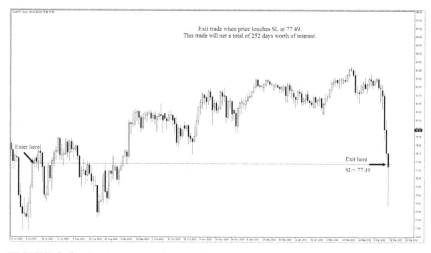

FIGURE 9.6 Trade Hits Breakeven After 36 Weeks

Once the position hits breakeven, there is no more risk for the trade. Swap is continuously earned for every day that the trade is open.

Short Trade Setup

We use the GBP/AUD on the daily time frame to illustrate the short setup. Here are the steps to execute the swap and fly strategy for short:

1. Identify a three black crows candlestick pattern. (See Figure 9.7.)
2. Enter short at the opening of the next candle.
3. Reference a recent significant high to set the stop loss. (See Figure 9.8.)
4. Once the market moves in your favor at a risk to reward ratio of 1:1, shift your stop loss to the entry price. (See Figure 9.9.)
5. Trade hits breakeven after 35 weeks (245 days). (See Figure 9.10.)

From the short example in Figure 9.10:

The swap for holding a short GBP/AUD position was AUD14 per standard lot, which was equivalent to 1.4 pips. The swap per week is 1.4 pips × 7 = 9.8 pips. The swap for 35 weeks is 9.8 pips × 35 = 343 pips.

Once the position hits breakeven, there is no more risk for the trade. Swap is continuously earned for every day that the trade is open.

FIGURE 9.7 Identify Three Black Crows Candlestick Pattern

Source: Created with FX Primus Ltd, a PRIME Mantle Corporation PLC company.

FIGURE 9.8 Set Stop Loss and Profit Target

Source: Created with FX Primus Ltd, a PRIME Mantle Corporation PLC company.

Strategy Roundup

On FXPRIMUS platform, short positions on GBP/AUD and long positions on AUD/JPY give the highest positive swaps. For maximum results on this strategy, it is prudent to choose the currency pairs that yield the highest

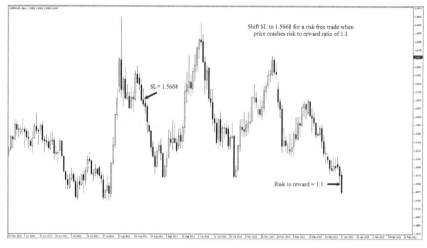

FIGURE 9.9   Stop Loss Shifted to Entry Price

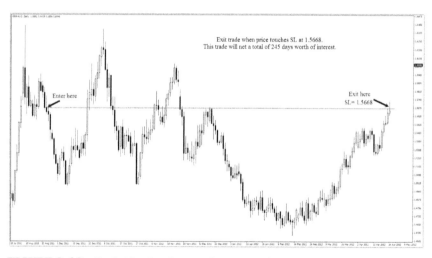

FIGURE 9.10   Trade Hits Breakeven After 35 Weeks

positive swap on the broker's platform. Do take note that swap rates are
not fixed. They move in tandem with central banks' rates.

Once the trades are executed, the first milestone is to shift the stop
loss to breakeven so that there is no more risk attached to the trade.

We then allow the trade to remain open every day until the new stop loss is hit. Doing this allows us to earn positive swap every day.

Traders can also choose to close this trade before it exits, provided the risk to reward ratio is favorable. As an example, traders can choose to exit the entire position totally if the risk to reward ratio yields a minimum factor of 1:3.

For the long AUD/JPY trade, the stop loss was 570 pips. Hence, traders could have chosen to exit the trade entirely if the AUD/JPY was at a minimum of 1710 pips (570 × 3) above the entry price.

For the short GBP/AUD trade, the stop loss was 725 pips. Hence, traders could have chosen to exit the trade entirely if the GBP/AUD was at a minimum of 2175 pips (725 × 3) below the entry price.

STRATEGY 13: COMMODITY CORRELATION (PART 1)

Oil is one of the world's basic necessities. Among other things, it is needed to run factories, plants, machinery, ships, and cars. A decline in oil prices is a nightmare for oil producers but a dream come true for oil consumers. The reverse is also true, when oil prices hit record highs. In July 2008, oil peaked at over USD147 a barrel. Those were the days when oil producers were smiling and oil consumers were sweating.

Canada is a country that exports most of its oil. In fact, as one of the world's top ten oil-producing nations, its economy is severely hit when oil prices decline. Many traders today also utilize the price of oil to predict the movement of the Canadian dollar.

When oil prices are high, the Canadian dollar tends to strengthen. When oil prices are low, the Canadian dollar tends to weaken. Japan, in contrast, is considered a net oil importer. This causes the Japanese yen to weaken considerably when oil prices are high and vice versa.

Many traders ask me for a "magic" strategy to trade oil. However, I don't particularly like to trade it because oil prices can be very volatile.

An easier improvisation of trading oil directly would be to utilize knowledge of oil prices to trade the CAD/JPY currency pair. As Canada is a net oil exporter and Japan is a net oil importer, the price of oil becomes a leading indicator for the movement of the CAD/JPY currency pair.

Time Frame

The commodity correlation method works with the daily charts (D1). This means that each candle on the chart represents 1 day of price movement.

Indicators

We use the average true range (ATR) indicator to set the stop loss for this strategy.

Average True Range   The ATR is an indicator developed by J. Welles Wilder to measure the volatility of the market. The true range is defined as the largest value of the absolute difference between the:

1. Current high and current low
2. Current high and the previous close
3. Current low and the previous close

   The ATR is an N-period exponential moving average of the true range. For example, ATR 14 is a 14-period exponential moving average of the true range.
   A larger value of ATR indicates a higher volatility, and a smaller value of ATR indicates a lower volatility. We will use the ATR as a guide to set our stop losses and profit targets.

Currency Pairs

This strategy is used with CAD/JPY only, with the movement of oil prices acting as a leading indicator.

Strategy Concept

The price movement on the oil chart is used as a reference to trigger a trade on the CAD/JPY. Technical levels of support and resistance on the oil chart are used to spot long and short trades on CAD/JPY. If candles close above resistance on the oil chart, a long trade is triggered on the CAD/JPY the following day. Similarly, if candles close below support on the oil chart, a short trade is triggered on the CAD/JPY the following day.
   The risk to reward ratio is set as 1:3. A bigger target is employed to allow the trade to run its course.

Long Trade Setup

Here are the steps to execute the commodity correlation strategy for long:

1. Identify the resistance of the oil chart on the daily time frame.
2. Identify a candle that closes above the resistance. (See Figure 9.11.)

FIGURE 9.11 Identify a Candle that Closes Above Resistance

FIGURE 9.12 Set Stop Loss and Profit Target

3. Enter long on CAD/JPY at the opening of the next day's candle.
4. Set the stop loss at twice the ATR of the previous candle, which is 154 pips (77×2).
5. Set the profit target at a risk to reward ratio of 1:3. In this example, the profit target is 462 pips (154×3). (See Figure 9.12.)

FIGURE 9.13   Trade Hits Profit Target

From the long example in Figure 9.13:

Entry price = 80.10
Stop loss = 78.56
Profit target = 84.72

The risk for this trade is 154 pips, and the reward is 462 pips if the profit target is hit. The risk to reward ratio would be 1:3, which yields a tidy 9% return if we take a 3% risk.

Short Trade Setup

Here are the steps to execute the commodity correlation strategy for short:

1. Identify the support of the oil chart on the daily time frame.
2. Identify a candle that closes below the support. (See Figure 9.14.)
3. Enter short on CAD/JPY at the opening of the next day's candle.
4. Set the stop loss at twice the ATR of the previous candle, which is 234 pips (117 × 2).
5. Set the profit target at a risk to reward ratio of 1:3. In this example, the profit target is 702 pips (234 × 3). (See Figure 9.15.)

FIGURE 9.14 Identify a Candle that Closes Below Support

FIGURE 9.15 Set Stop Loss and Profit Target

From the short example in Figure 9.16:

$$\text{Entry price} = 80.34$$
$$\text{Stop loss} = 82.68$$
$$\text{Profit target} = 73.32$$

FIGURE 9.16   Trade Hits Profit Target

The risk for this trade is 154 pips, and the reward is 462 pips if the profit target is hit. The risk to reward ratio is 1:3, which yields a tidy 9% return if we take a 3% risk.

STRATEGY 13: COMMODITY CORRELATION (PART 2)

The correlation coefficient is a number that describes the extent to which two instruments are correlated to each other. The number oscillates between −1 and +1.

Commonly mistaken as a momentum oscillator, the correlation coefficient is instead a number that moves from periods of positive correlation to periods of negative correlation. Located on one end of the spectrum, +1 is considered a state of perfect positive correlation between the two instruments. If the number is anywhere between 0 and +1, the two instruments move in the same direction but with varying degrees of positive correlation.

On the other end of the spectrum, −1 is considered a state of perfect negative correlation between the two instruments. If the number is anywhere between 0 and −1, the two instruments move in the opposite direction but with varying degrees of negative correlation.

For much of 2011 and 2012, the correlation coefficient for gold and the dollar index was between −0.6 and −0.8. This means that if the dollar index was up, there was a 60% to 80% probability that gold prices would come down.

In contrast, if the dollar index was down, there was a 60% to 80% probability that gold prices would go up.

Here we explore how to trade spot gold using the U.S. Dollar Index as a reference. The U.S. Dollar Index is an exchange-traded index that represents the value of the U.S. dollar in terms of a basket of six major foreign currencies. These are:

Euro (57.6%)

Japanese yen (13.6%)

UK pound (11.9%)

Canadian dollar (9.1%)

Swedish krona (4.2%)

Swiss franc (3.6%)

The price action of the dollar index gives us an idea of how the U.S. economy is performing compared to other major world economies.

On August 15, 1971, the United States unilaterally terminated the Bretton Woods system of having the U.S. dollar pegged to gold at USD35 an ounce. At the same time, the U.S. dollar became a reserve currency.

The U.S. Dollar Index was started in March 1973. Its beginning value was 100.000.

Historically, from 1967 until 2012, the Dollar Index averaged 98.51, reaching a historical high of 164.72 in February 1985 and a low of 70.698 on March 16, 2008, during the global financial crisis.

Gold prices, however, have steadily been climbing. The end of 2011 marked the eleventh straight year of gold's spectacular bull run, hitting a record high of USD1920 an ounce on September 16, 2011.

This strategy seeks to exploit the inverse relationship between the Dollar Index and the price of gold. According to the World Gold Council, "While holding all else equal, gold tends to rise when the US dollar falls."

In November 2010, Federal Reserve chairman Ben Bernanke announced a second round of quantitative easing (QE2) by injecting USD600 billion into the financial system. The added supply of US dollars in the system caused gold prices to hit record highs within a month.

In September 2012, in a move widely touted as "QE3," the Federal Reserve said it would expand its holdings of long-term securities with open-ended purchases of USD40 billion of mortgage debt a month. The announcement caused the price of gold to hit a 7-month high. With central banks worldwide taking unprecedented measures to ensure ample liquidity in the global financial system, the inverse relationship between the Dollar Index and gold prices looks set to continue.

Let's see how this strategy works.

Time Frame

The commodity correlation strategy works with the daily candle (D1). This means that each candle on the chart represents 1 day of price movement.

Indicators

We use the ATR indicator.

Currency Pairs

Use spot gold or XAU/USD only, with the price action of the Dollar Index as a leading indicator.

Strategy Concept

The price action of the Dollar Index is used as a reference to trigger a trade on the XAU/USD. Technical levels of support and resistance on the Dollar Index chart are used to spot long and short trades on XAU/USD. If a candle closes below support on the Dollar Index chart, a long trade is triggered on the XAU/USD the following day. Similarly, if a candle closes above resistance on the Dollar Index chart, a short trade is triggered on the XAU/USD the following day.

The risk to reward ratio is set as 1:3. A bigger target is employed to allow the trade to run its course.

Long Trade Setup

Here are the steps to execute the commodity correlation strategy for long:

1. Identify the support of the Dollar Index chart on the daily time frame.
2. Identify a candle that closes below the support. (See Figure 9.17.)
3. Enter long on gold (XAU/USD) at the opening of the next day's candle.
4. Set the stop loss at twice the ATR as the previous candle, which is 2,664 pips (1,332 × 2).
5. Set the profit target at a risk to reward ratio of 1:3. In this example, the profit target is 7,992 pips (2664 × 3). (See Figure 9.18.)

From the short example in Figure 9.19:

$$\text{Entry price} = 1291.23$$
$$\text{Stop loss} = 1264.59$$
$$\text{Profit target} = 1371.15$$

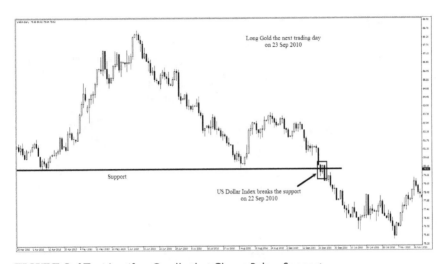

FIGURE 9.17 Identify a Candle that Closes Below Support

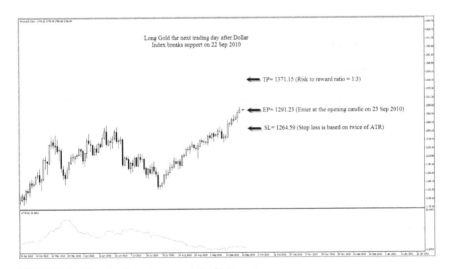

FIGURE 9.18 Set Stop Loss and Profit Target

The risk for this trade is 2,664 pips, and the reward is 7,992 pips if the profit target is hit. The risk to reward ratio is 1:3, which yields a tidy 9% return if we take a 3% risk.

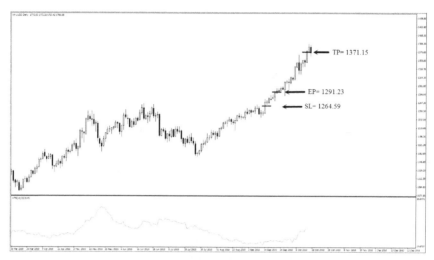

FIGURE 9.19   Trade Hits Profit Target

Short Trade Setup

Here are the steps to execute the commodity correlation for short:

1. Identify the resistance of the Dollar Index chart on the daily time frame.
2. Identify a candle that closes above the resistance. (See Figure 9.20.)
3. Enter short on gold (XAU/USD) at the opening of the next day's candle.
4. Set the stop loss at twice the ATR as of the previous candle, which is 8,044 pips (4,022 × 2).
5. Set the profit target at a risk to reward ratio of 1:3. In this example, the profit target is 24,132 pips (8,044 × 3). (See Figure 9.21.)

From the short example in Figure 9.22:

$$\text{Entry price} = 1857.81$$
$$\text{Stop loss} = 1938.25$$
$$\text{Profit target} = 1616.49$$

The risk for this trade is 8,044 pips, and the reward is 24,132 pips if the profit target is hit. The risk to reward ratio is 1:3, which yields a tidy 9% return if we take a 3% risk.

FIGURE 9.20 Identify a Candle that Closes Above Resistance

Source: Created with FX Primus Ltd, a PRIME Mantle Corporation PLC company. All rights reserved.

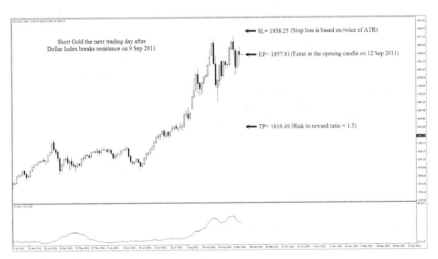

FIGURE 9.21 Set Stop Loss and Profit Target

Source: Created with FX Primus Ltd, a PRIME Mantle Corporation PLC company. All rights reserved.

Strategy Roundup

Part of the commodity correlation strategy seeks to take advantage of the positive correlation between oil prices and the CAD/JPY currency pair. Using oil prices as a reference, trades are triggered on the CAD/JPY. This strategy is especially suited to traders who would like to trade oil but prefer not to experience the volatility associated with it.

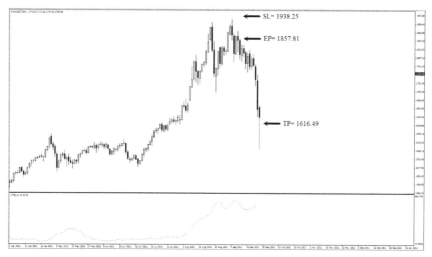

FIGURE 9.22   Trade Hits Profit Target
Source: Created with FX Primus Ltd, a PRIME Mantle Corporation PLC company. All rights reserved.

Part 2 of the commodity correlation strategy seeks to take advantage of the negative correlation between the Dollar Index and gold prices. Using the Dollar Index as a reference, trades are triggered on XAU/USD, which is the price for spot gold on FXPRIMUS.

With the Federal Reserve announcing its plans to keep interest rates low until the middle of 2015, the inverse relationship between the U.S. dollar and gold prices looks set to remain. This strategy is ideal for gold traders all around the world because it provides an objective way to take an entry for gold, using the Dollar Index as an important reference.

STRATEGY 14: SIAMESE TWINS

In late 2007, China overtook Japan to become Australia's largest trading partner. In 2009, China became Australia's largest export market, consuming commodities such as iron ore, coal, gas, and wool in record amounts.

According to Australia's department of Foreign Affairs and Trade, Australia's total trade with China in 2010 was $105 billion, almost 24% more than the previous year. It was the first time that Australia's two-way trade with a single nation topped the $100 billion level. Forty years ago, two-way trade between China and Australia was less than $100 million.

For this reason alone, Australia's economy tends to move in tandem with China's economy. When China reports good numbers on the Purchasing Managers Index (PMI), gross domestic product (GDP) or the trade balance, Australia's currency tends to rise. Similarly, when China reports disappointing figures, the Australian dollar tends to fall as well.

This strategy seeks to take advantage of the movement of the AUD/USD by taking cue from China's reported figures and monetary policies. It is especially useful since we are not able to freely trade the Chinese currency (yuan) yet.

Time Frame

The Siamese twins method works with the daily candle (D1). This means that each candle on the chart represents 1 day of price movement.

Indicators

No indicators are used for this strategy.

Currency Pairs

This strategy is applicable only to AUD/USD.

Strategy Concept

When China announces good data, such as high GDP and high PMI numbers, the AUD tends to strengthen for two reasons.

1. China will start to import more raw materials from Australia. This increase in business gives rise to a stronger AUD because China has to pay for such materials in AUD.

2. Good data from China tend to increase speculation on higher-yielding currencies. This is because China is largely seen as a major global player, and good numbers from China tend to have a knock-on effect on the world economy. This positive effect on the global economy encourages the appetite for risk, which in turn strengthens the AUD because its interest rate remains one of the highest among the G20 nations.

We take a long position on AUD/USD immediately after China announces better-than-expected data. Similarly, we take a short position on AUD/USD immediately after China announces worse-than-expected data.

I call this strategy Siamese twins because the economies of China and Australia are joined at the hip. When China does well, the Australian economy flourishes, and vice versa.

Long Trade Setup

Here are the steps to execute the Siamese twins strategy for long:

1. Look for any major news from China. On November 30, 2010, we see how China cut the banks' reserve requirement ratio for the first time in three years. This frees up more cash, which encourages banks to lend. The effect is seen as positive because it spurs economic growth in China.
2. Go long on AUD/USD immediately. (See Figure 9.23.)
3. Set the stop loss below the previous low.
4. The trade will have two profit targets with a risk to reward ratio of 1:1 and 1:2 respectively. (See Figure 9.24.)

From the long example in Figure 9.25:

$$\text{Entry price} = 1.0000$$
$$\text{Stop loss} = 0.9600$$
$$\text{Profit target 1} = 1.0400$$
$$\text{Profit target 2} = 1.0800$$

FIGURE 9.23   News Release

FIGURE 9.24 Set Stop Loss and Profit Targets

FIGURE 9.25 Trade Hits Profit Targets

The risk for this trade is 400 pips, and the reward is 800 pips if both targets are hit. The risk to reward ratio is 1:2, which yields a 6% return if we take a 3% risk.

Short Trade Setup

Here are the steps to execute the Siamese twins strategy for short:

1. Look out for any major news from China. In this example, we see how the actual number of China's HSBC flash manufacturing PMI is worse than expected. The effect is seen as negative because it is viewed as a contraction in China's economy.
2. Go short on AUD/USD immediately. (See Figure 9.26.)
3. Set the stop loss above the previous high.
4. The trade has two profit targets with risk to reward ratios of 1:1 and 1:2 respectively. (See Figure 9.27.)

From the long example in Figure 9.28:

$$\text{Entry price} = 1.0458$$
$$\text{Stop loss} = 1.0638$$
$$\text{Profit target 1} = 1.0278$$
$$\text{Profit target 2} = 1.0098$$

FIGURE 9.26   News Release

Source: Created with FX Primus Ltd, a PRIME Mantle Corporation PLC company. All rights reserved.

FIGURE 9.27 Set Stop Loss and Profit Targets

FIGURE 9.28 Trade Hits Profit Targets

The risk for this trade is 180 pips, and the reward is 360 pips respectively if both targets are hit. The risk to reward ratio is 1:2, which yields a 6% return if we take a 3% risk.

Strategy Roundup

The Siamese twins strategy is perfect for position traders because of the long time frame employed. When China announces news—either good or bad—the subsequent effect on the Australian economy may take weeks or even months to play out.

As we learned in the swap and fly strategy, a long AUD/USD trade can give you additional swap as well. This amount can be very significant if the trade is held for several months before it is exited.

CHAPTER 10

Strategies for Mechanical Traders

As a mechanical trader, your main focus in trading the markets is not time driven but system driven. Your trades are based on a fixed routine, regardless of time frame and regardless of market activity.

This style of trading is especially suited to newbies because strategy execution is based purely on a set of fixed steps or rules. Due to its non-dependence on specific time frames, the three strategies discussed here employ time frames that span three different categories: scalping, day trading, and position trading.

The first strategy, the guppy burst, is based on the 5-minute (M5) chart. The second strategy, English breakfast tea, is based on the 15-minute (M15) chart. The third strategy, good morning Asia, is based on the daily (D1) chart.

Many newbies love the fixed routine by which mechanical trades are set up. It is also the reason why many go on to develop automated trading systems by coding the trading rules into software.

Let's have a look at all three strategies.

STRATEGY 15: GUPPY BURST

The first step in developing a mechanical trading system is to understand and describe market behavior. The next step is to figure out the rules for entries and exits. The guppy burst seeks to exploit trading profits when the market is quiet.

There is a window of around three hours between the close of the U.S. market and the opening of the Asian market. The forex market is relatively quiet during this time and tends to move in a gentle yet predictable manner.

The market then springs to life again when the Asian market opens. The guppy burst seeks to identify the trading range during this 3-hour window and anticipate a potential breakout of the trading range.

To take full advantage of this potential breakout, I have selected one of the most volatile crosses, the GBP/JPY, commonly known as the guppy among forex traders.

Time Frame

The guppy burst method works with the 5-minute candle (M5). This means that each candle represents 5 minutes of price movement.

Indicators

We use only pure price action; no indicators are used for this strategy.

Currency Pairs

The guppy burst method applies only to the GBP/JPY.

Strategy Concept

After the trading range is identified, we place pending long and pending short orders. The entry price for the pending long is at the resistance level while the stop loss is located at the support level. The entry price for the pending short is at the support level while the stop loss is at the resistance level.

The profit target is set at twice the amount of the stop loss. As an example, if the stop loss is 50 pips from the entry price, the profit target will be 100 pips. This is a risk to reward ratio of 1:2.

Long Trade Setup

The reference candle for this strategy is the one that corresponds to 5 P.M. New York time, which is the closing time of the U.S. market. This is the 00:00-hour candle on the FXPRIMUS platform.

Here are the steps to execute the guppy burst strategy for long:

1. Identify the trading range in the first three hours after the U.S. market closes by referencing the highest high (resistance) and the lowest low (support) in these three hours. (See Figure 10.1.)
2. Place a pending buy stop order with entry price at the highest high (resistance).

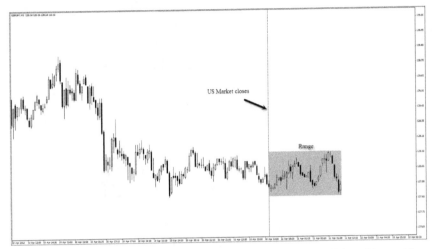

FIGURE 10.1 Identify Trading Range by Referencing Highest High and Lowest Low

Source: Created with FX Primus Ltd, a PRIME Mantle Corporation PLC company.

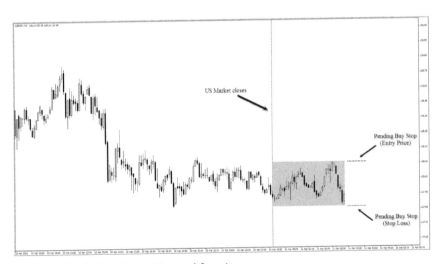

FIGURE 10.2 Set Entry Price and Stop Loss

Source: Created with FX Primus Ltd, a PRIME Mantle Corporation PLC company.

3. Set the stop loss at the lowest low (support). (See Figure 10.2.)

4. Measure the number of pips between the EP and SL. The profit target is double that number of pips. In this example, the number of pips between EP (128.16) and SL (127.86) is 30, so the TP will be 60 pips above the EP at 128.76. (See Figure 10.3.)

FIGURE 10.3 Engage Pending Buy Stop

Source: Created with FX Primus Ltd, a PRIME Mantle Corporation PLC company. All rights reserved.

FIGURE 10.4 Trade Hits Profit Target

Source: Created with FX Primus Ltd, a PRIME Mantle Corporation PLC company. All rights reserved.

From the long example in Figure 10.4:

$$Entry\ price = 128.16$$
$$Stop\ loss = 127.86$$
$$Profit\ target = 128.76$$

The risk for this trade is 30 pips, and the reward is 60 pips. The risk to reward ratio is 1:2, which yields a tidy 6% return if we take a 3% risk.

Short Trade Setup

The reference candle for this strategy is the one that corresponds to 5 P.M. New York time, which is the closing time of the U.S. market. This is the 00:00-hour candle on the FXPRIMUS platform.

Here are the steps to execute the guppy burst strategy for short:

1. Identify the trading range in the first three hours after the U.S. market closes by referencing the highest high (resistance) and the lowest low (support) in these three hours. (See Figure 10.5.)
2. Place a pending sell stop order with entry price at the lowest low (support).
3. Set the stop loss at the highest high (resistance). (See Figure 10.6.)
4. Measure the number of pips between the EP and SL. The profit target is double that number of pips. In this example, the number of pips between EP (128.12) and SL (128.33) is 21, so the TP will be 42 pips below the EP at 127.70. (See Figure 10.7.)

From the short example in Figure 10.8:

$$\text{Entry price} = 128.12$$
$$\text{Stop loss} = 128.33$$
$$\text{Profit target} = 127.70$$

The risk for this trade is 21 pips, and the reward is 42 pips. The risk to reward ratio is 1:2, which yields a tidy 6% return if we take a 3% risk.

FIGURE 10.5 Identify Trading Range by Referencing Highest High and Lowest Low

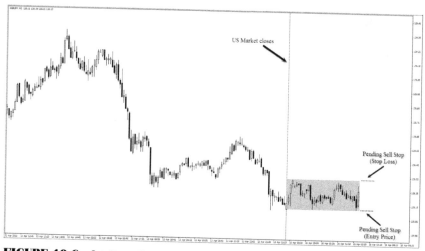

FIGURE 10.6   Set Entry Price and Stop Loss

Source: Created with FX Primus Ltd, a PRIME Mantle Corporation PLC company. All rights reserved.

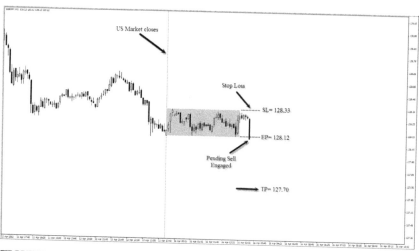

FIGURE 10.7   Engage Pending Sell Stop

Source: Created with FX Primus Ltd, a PRIME Mantle Corporation PLC company. All rights reserved.

Strategy Roundup

As there is no way to anticipate when the market will reach the entry price, the best option is to create one pending long order and one pending short order after you have identified the trading range of the three-hour window.

Once either of the pending orders is triggered, delete the other pending order immediately. As an example, if the pending long order gets

FIGURE 10.8 Trade Hits Profit Target

triggered first, delete the pending short order. If the pending short order gets triggered first, delete the pending long order.

This strategy is suitable for traders who are available during a specific time of the day to execute the trade during the three-hour gap.

STRATEGY 16: ENGLISH BREAKFAST TEA

When traders trade a particular currency pair for a long period of time, they may start to observe certain characteristics or behaviors of that currency pair. These characteristics or behaviors could happen during market opening hours, market closing hours, major news releases, Christmas and New Year holidays, financial year closings, and so on.

In my years of trading, I have noticed peculiar behaviors in various currency pairs. In this strategy, I share one of my observations about the GBP/USD during the London opening hours.

Time Frame

The English breakfast tea method works with the 15-minute candle (M15). This means that each candle represents 15 minutes of price movement.

Indicators

We use pure price action, and no indicators are used for this strategy.

Currency Pair

This strategy is applied to the GBP/USD only.

Strategy Concept

The English breakfast tea strategy is based on an observation I've had on the GBP/USD for a while now. This occurs before and after the London market opens in the morning.

Here's what I discovered: When the GBP/USD trends in one direction from 04:15 hours to 08:30 hours London time, it has a tendency to move in the other direction after 08:30 hours.

Hence, we first compare the closing price of the 15-minute (M15) candle that corresponds to 04:15 hours and 08:15 hours London time to determine the direction of the GBP/USD. We then enter a trade in the opposite direction at 08:30 hours London time.

As an example, if the closing price of the M15 candle at 08:15 hours is lower than the closing price at 04:15 hours, we go long at 08:30 hours. If the closing price of the M15 candle at 08:15 hours is higher than the closing price at 04:15 hours, we go short at 08:30 hours.

The stop loss is fixed at 30 pips, and there are three profit targets for this strategy with risk to reward ratios of 1:1, 1:2, and 1:3. In other words, the profit targets are 30 pips, 60 pips, and 90 pips respectively.

Long Trade Setup

The 10:30-hour candle of the charts on FXPRIMUS platform is used to illustrate this strategy because it corresponds to London time 08:30 hours.

Here are the steps to execute the English breakfast tea for long:

1. The closing price of the M15 candle at 10:15 hours must be lower than the closing price at 06:15. (See Figure 10.9.)
2. Enter at the opening of the candle at 10:30 hours. This is the entry price.
3. Set the stop loss at 30 pips below the entry price.
4. There are three profit targets at 30 pips, 60 pips, and 90 pips above the EP respectively. (See Figure 10.10.)

From the long example in Figure 10.11:

$$\text{Entry price} = 1.5900$$
$$\text{Stop loss} = 1.5870$$
$$\text{Profit target } 1 = 1.5930$$

$$\text{Profit target } 2 = 1.5960$$
$$\text{Profit target } 3 = 1.5990$$

The risk for this trade is 30 pips, and the reward is 90 pips if all three targets are hit. The risk to reward ratio is 1:3, which yields a tidy 9% return if we take a 3% risk.

FIGURE 10.9 Closing Price at 10:15 Hours Must Be Lower than Closing Price at 06:15 Hours

Source: Created with FX Primus Ltd, a PRIME Mantle Corporation PLC company. All rights reserved.

FIGURE 10.10 Three Profit Targets at 30 Pips, 60 Pips, and 90 Pips Above Entry Price

Source: Created with FX Primus Ltd, a PRIME Mantle Corporation PLC company. All rights reserved.

FIGURE 10.11   Trade Hits Profit Targets

Short Trade Setup

The 10:30-hour candle of the charts on FXPRIMUS platform is used to illustrate this strategy because it corresponds to London time 08:30 hours.
    Here are the steps to execute the English breakfast tea for short:

1. The closing price of the M15 candle at 10:15 hours must be higher than the closing price at 06:15 hours. (See Figure 10.12.)
2. Enter at the opening of the candle at 10:30 hours. This is the entry price.
3. Set the stop loss at 30 pips above the entry price.
4. There will be three profit targets at 30 pips, 60 pips, and 90 pips below the EP respectively. (See Figure 10.13.)

From the short example in Figure 10.14:

$$\text{Entry price} = 1.5819$$
$$\text{Stop loss} = 1.5849$$
$$\text{Profit target 1} = 1.5789$$
$$\text{Profit target 2} = 1.5759$$
$$\text{Profit target 3} = 1.5729$$

The risk for this trade is 30 pips, and the reward is 90 pips if all three targets are hit. The risk to reward ratio is 1:3, which yields a tidy 9% return if we take a 3% risk.

FIGURE 10.12 Closing Price at 10:15 Hours Must Be Higher than Closing Price at 06:15 Hours

Source: Created with FX Primus Ltd, a PRIME Mantle Corporation PLC company. All rights reserved.

FIGURE 10.13 Three Profit Targets at 30 Pips, 60 Pips, and 90 Pips Below the Entry Price

Source: Created with FX Primus Ltd, a PRIME Mantle Corporation PLC company. All rights reserved.

Strategy Roundup

This strategy is based on a fixed time period every day, specifically geared towards the opening of the London market. The rules are simple and specific because there is no confusion as to the direction of the trade. Going

FIGURE 10.14 Trade Hits Profit Targets

long or short is the first step that new traders normally get confused on when they begin discretionary trading.

With its clear-cut rules and mechanical execution, the English breakfast tea method eliminates the guesswork in terms of strategy direction.

STRATEGY 17: GOOD MORNING ASIA

A fair number of traders prefer to trade the U.S. and Europe sessions of the forex market because they feel that the market tends to be more exciting at those times. These traders consider the Asian session boring and quiet most of the time.

However, many part-time retail traders who are based in the United States and Europe miss out trading opportunities in the U.S. and Europe sessions because of work or business commitments. The only time they can trade happens to fall within the perceived boring and quiet Asia session.

Thankfully, now we all know that the forex market is open 24 hours a day. When there are trade-related activities, there are opportunities.

My last strategy of this book is traded on the early-morning Asian hours. This time period can provide numerous opportunities for traders located in different time zones across the world, whether they are part time or full time. I hope that it will greet you like the bright morning sun.

Time Frame

The good morning Asia strategy works with the daily candle (D1). This means that each candle represents 1 day of price movement.

Indicators

We use only pure price action, and no indicators are used for this strategy.

Currency Pairs

This strategy applies only to the USD/JPY.

Strategy Concept

Opening hours of the Asian market begin after the U.S. market closes. The direction of the Asian market tends to take its cue from the previous day's performance on the U.S. market because the U.S. market is the largest economy in the world.

If the U.S. market closes with a bullish sentiment, the Asian market usually starts the day bullish. If the U.S. market closes with a bearish sentiment, the Asian market usually starts off bearish.

During the early-morning Asian hours, the best currency pair to take advantage of this phenomenon is none other than the USD/JPY, as the Japanese yen is the only Asian major currency.

This strategy allows you to position yourself just before the opening of the Asian market—hence the name good morning Asia.

The entry time of this strategy is right after the U.S. market closes at 5 P.M. If the previous daily candle is a bull candle, we ride along the momentum to go long on Asia opening. If the previous daily candle is a bear candle, we follow the bearish flow with a short on Asia opening.

We take the low or high of the previous candle as the stop loss. The risk to reward for this strategy is 2:1. If the stop loss is 80 pips, the profit target is 40 pips.

Long Trade Setup

For this strategy, the opening and closing of the daily candle corresponds to 5 P.M. New York time, which is the closing time of the U.S. market.

Here are the steps to execute the good morning Asia strategy for long:

1. Ensure that the previous day's candle is a bull candle (i.e., the closing price of the candle is higher than the opening price). (See Figure 10.15.)

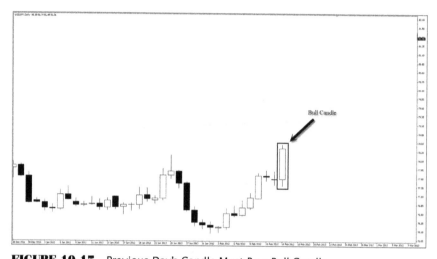

FIGURE 10.15   Previous Day's Candle Must Be a Bull Candle
Source: Created with FX Primus Ltd, a PRIME Mantle Corporation PLC company. All rights reserved.

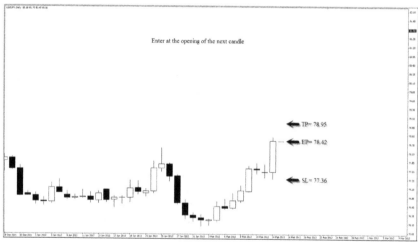

FIGURE 10.16   Set Stop Loss and Profit Targets
Source: Created with FX Primus Ltd, a PRIME Mantle Corporation PLC company. All rights reserved.

2. Enter at the opening of the next candle. This is the entry price.
3. Set the stop loss at the low of the previous day's candle.
4. Measure the number of pips between the entry price and stop loss. If the number of pips is less than 30, shift the stop loss lower to make sure it is at least 30 pips from the entry price. The profit target is half that number of pips. In this example, the number of pips between entry

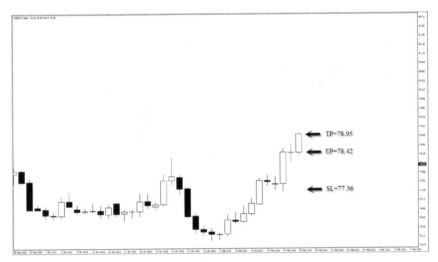

FIGURE 10.17 Trade Hits Profit Target

Source: Created with FX Primus Ltd, a PRIME Mantle Corporation PLC company. All rights reserved.

price (78.42) and stop loss (77.36) is 106, so the profit target is 53 pips above the entry price at 78.95. (See Figure 10.16.)

From the long example in Figure 10.17:

$$\text{Entry price} = 78.42$$
$$\text{Stop loss} = 77.36$$
$$\text{Profit target} = 78.95$$

The risk for this trade is 106 pips, and the reward is 53 pips. The risk to reward ratio is 2:1, which yields a 1.5% return if we take a 3% risk.

Short Trade Setup

Here are the steps to execute the good morning Asia strategy for short:

1. Ensure that the previous day's candle is a bear candle (i.e., the closing price of the candle is lower than the opening price). (See Figure 10.18.)
2. Enter at the opening of the next candle. This is the entry price.
3. Set the stop loss at the high of the previous day's candle.
4. Measure the number of pips between the entry price and stop loss. If the number of pips is less than 30, shift the stop loss higher to make sure it is at least 30 pips from the entry price. The profit target is half of that number of pips. In this example, the number of pips between

FIGURE 10.18   Previous Day's Candle Must Be a Bear Candle

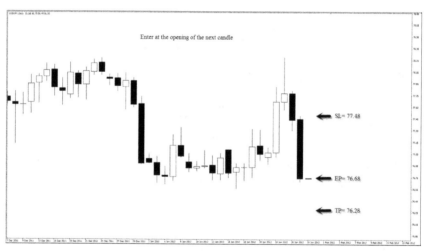

FIGURE 10.19   Set Stop Loss and Profit Target

entry price (76.68) and stop loss (77.48) is 80 pips, so the profit target is 40 pips below the entry price at 76.28. (See Figure 10.19.)

From the short example in Figure 10.20:

Entry price = 76.68
Stop loss = 77.48
Profit target = 76.28

FIGURE 10.20   Trade Hits Profit Target

Source: Created with FX Primus Ltd, a PRIME Mantle Corporation PLC company. All rights reserved.

The risk for this trade is 80 pips, and the reward is 40 pips. The risk to reward ratio is 2:1, which yields a 1.5% return if we take a 3% risk.

Strategy Roundup

This strategy is suitable for traders with very little time to monitor the market. Furthermore, it does not require any complex market analysis. The entry time is predictable because the market is entered at a fixed time of the day, every single day.

Good morning Asia centers on the USD/JPY for three reasons:

1. The United States and Japan are the largest and third largest economies in the world respectively.

2. The USD/JPY is the second most traded currency pair in the world, right after the EUR/USD.

3. Japan is the first country in Asia where markets open. Hence, ample liquidity on the USD/JPY allows traders to execute long and short positions easily.

CHAPTER 11

Conclusion

You now have in your hands the tools to help you carve out a very profitable trading career in the forex market. The path is simple: Determine your dominant trading style, and employ strategies specific to that style.

If you are a scalper, stick to the rapid-fire or piranha strategies outlined in Chapter 6. If you are a day trader, either one of the four strategies discussed in Chapter 7 will give you lasting success. If you are a swing trader, following the trend rider or the power ranger is an absolute must.

Trading is simple but it's not easy. It's simple because there are only a few rules to follow—five to be exact. Here they are:

1. **Ensure the correct time frame.** Be careful to check the time frame on your trading platform before you trigger a trade. An uptrend on the hourly chart may be a downtrend on the daily chart. Also, the strategies discussed in this book are specific to certain time frames, so pay extra attention to the time frame before you fire off a trade.

2. **Overlay the necessary indicators.** Some strategies require the use of indicators. Remember to check that the indicators have the correct settings. Failure to check could give rise to a false setup. If you are using the Meta Trader 4 trading platform, make use of the template feature, which allows you to save various customized templates with the required indicators.

3. **Execute long or short based on the strategy rules.** Take note that while the market may give you a setup, you are allowed to trigger a trade only if all the rules fit. Some strategies may have three steps while others have five. You must be strict and trigger a long or short trade only when all rules are met.

4. **Double check your entry point, stop loss, and profit target levels.** Some traders get excited when they see a setup and hurriedly enter trades. Ensure that your entry point, stop loss, and profit target levels are set according to the rules of the specific strategy. Don't worry if you make a mistake—the Meta Trader 4 platform has a button called "Modify Order" that allows you to alter these levels should you make any prior mistakes.

5. **Record your results in your trading journal.** This is a good habit to form early in your trading career. A trading journal is basically a diary that helps you to archive the trades that you have taken. A good trading journal should include columns for you to input the trade entries and exits and also space for you to record your emotions before, during, and after the trade.

These five rules apply across the board, regardless of which category you are in: scalper, day trader, swing trader, position trader, or mechanical trader.

Follow these five rules conscientiously and you will be on your way to becoming consistently profitable. That's the simple part. However, trading isn't easy. It's not easy because the only person who can stop you from achieving success in the forex market is you.

I would like to share one final lesson from my Chinese mentor to illustrate my point better. He taught me that getting from where we are now to where we want to go is a function of only three steps—yes, "just" three steps.

The first step is knowledge. Knowledge is defined as an awareness or understanding gained through education or experience. In forex, this step involves reading a forex quote, knowing how to execute a long or short trade, gaining clarity on the factors that move the markets, and developing insight into your very own trading profile. This knowledge is thoroughly discussed in Part One of this book, specifically in Chapters 1 through 5.

The second step is action. Action is defined as the art of applying knowledge through organized activities to achieve a desired result. In forex, this step involves watching the markets, studying the rules, executing the trade, and recording the results. This action is clearly detailed in Part Two of this book, in Chapters 6 through 10.

The third step starts with the letter "d." When I ask the audience in my seminars to guess what word this is, many people say decision, discipline, or determination. Although these are good traits, the answer is not in any of them.

The answer is *desire*.

What is the definition of desire? This is my mentor's definition:

如果我不能，我就一定要。如果我一定要，我就一定能。

In English, this means: "If I can't, then I must. If I must, then I can."

Any good forex mentor will be able to give you the functional ingredients of knowledge and action. Unfortunately, no mentor can give you desire. That has to come from deep inside you.

In the beginning of my story, I shared with you that I'm not a smart guy. I don't have a finance or economics degree. But what I had was the desire to succeed.

Do you have the absolute desire to be a mega trading success? If your answer is a resounding yes, congratulations, my friend. Because the other two ingredients of knowledge and action are found between the covers of this book.

It is my sincere wish that you enjoyed reading this book as much as I have enjoyed writing it. If you allow me, I will be your mentor to guide your every step on this fascinating journey. Whether you're a beginner or an advanced trader, my message remains the same: You can't afford to ignore the forex market anymore.

If you're a beginner, you might wonder how much time you need per day to master this skill. The answer is just one to two hours. The forex market is open 24 hours a day. You can start right now, without making any change to your present lifestyle. When you start, I'll guarantee you one thing: Within a few short years of seemingly not changing anything, you will end up changing everything.

My friend, the forex market is not just the largest financial market in the world. It is the biggest mirror to your soul. How you trade tells you who you really are.

So let's get started.

Let's play flat out.

Let's make magic.

Sincerely,
Mario Singh

Bibliography

"Australia Lowers Rate to 4.5% in a Bid to Boost Growth," *BBC News Business*, November 1, 2011. www.bbc.co.uk/news/business-15532567

Bank for International Settlement. *Triennial Central Bank Survey of Foreign Exchange and Derivatives Market Activity*. Monetary and Economic Department, December 2010.

Bennett, Allison, and Candice Zachariahs. "Yen Drops Versus Dollar, Euro After Bank of Japan Intervention," *Bloomberg Businessweek*, August 5, 2011. www .businessweek.com/news/2011–08–04/yen-drops-versus-dollar-euro-after-bank-of-japan-intervention.html

Braithwaite, Tom. "MF Global Files for Bankruptcy," *Financial Services*, October 31, 2011. www.ft.com/intl/cms/s/0/ba26dc98–036e-11e1–899a-00144feabdc0.html

Charlton, Emma. "Pound Rises as Spending Data Boosts Economic Outlook," *Bloomberg Businessweek*, February 24, 2012. www.businessweek.com/news/ 2012–02–24/pound-rises-as-spending-data-boosts-economic-outlook-gilts-gain .html

"China Cuts Banks' Reserve Requirement Ratios," CNBC, Reuters, February 18, 2012. www.cnbc.com/id/46438510/China_Cuts_Banks_Reserve_Requirement_Ratios

"Christchurch Earthquake Weakens NZD-Westpac," *RTT News*, Global Financial Newswires, February 22, 2011. www.rttnews.com/1558037/christchurch-earth quake-weakens-nzd-westpac.aspx

"Dollar Surges Against Yen on Japan Intervention," Channelnewsasia, Business News, October 31, 2011. www.channelnewsasia.com/stories/afp_asiapacific_ business/view/1162659/1/.html

"Egypt Pound Falls to 6-Year Low after Protests," *Reuters Africa*, January 26, 2011. http://af.reuters.com/article/investingNews/idAFJOE70P08220110126

Garnham, Peter, and Haig Simonian. "SNB Stuns Market with Franc Action," *Financial Times* Currencies, September 6, 2011. www.ft.com/intl/cms/s/0/ f5a361ce-d862–11e0–8f0a-00144feabdc0.html#axzz1uAhZMrQx

Greil, Anita, and John Revill. "Swiss Companies Struggle to Offset Pain of Strong Franc," *Wall Street Journal*, July 26, 2011. http://online.wsj.com/article/SB1000 1424053111904888304576474201727957350.html

Heath, Michael. "RBA Cuts Key Rate, Citing Risk Europe to Slow Global Growth," *Bloomberg Businessweek*, December 6, 2011. www.businessweek.com/news/ 2011–12–06/rba-cuts-key-rate-citing-risk- europe-to-slow-global-growth.html

Ho, Yudith. "Rupiah Weakens, Thai Stocks Fall After Indonesian Quake," *Bloomberg Businessweek*, April 11, 2012. www.bloomberg.com/news/2012–04–11/thai-stocks-fall-as-quake-prompts-tsunami-alerts-tin-rises.html

"Instant View: China Rises Interest Rates for 3rd Time in 2011," *Reuters*, July 6, 2011. www.reuters.com/article/2011/07/06/us-china-rates-iv-idUSTRE7651 JK20110706

Isidore, Chris. "European Central Bank Cuts Rates," CNNMoney, November 3, 2011. http://money.cnn.com/2011/11/03/news/international/ecb/index.htm

Nakamichi, Takashi. "Japan Officials Hint at Forex Intervention," *Wall Street Journal*, August 2, 2011. ttp://online.wsj.com/article/SB1000142405311190334 1404576482890699000396.html

Ondaatjie, Anusha. "Sri Lanka Raises Rates for the First Time in Five Years," *Bloomberg Businessweek*, February 2, 2012. www.businessweek.com/news/2012–02–02/sri-lanka-raises-rates-for-the-first-time-in-five-years.html

Oprita, Antonia. "ECB Cuts Rate, Relaxes Some Rules to Boost Liquidity". www.cnbc.com/id/45594288/ECB_Cuts_Rate_Relaxes_Some_Rules_to_Boost_Liquidity

Sprach Analyst. "People's Bank of China Raises Reserve Requirement Ratio by 50bpp" *Business Insider*, May 12, 2011. http://articles.businessinsider.com/2011–05–12/markets/30012832_1_reserve-requirement-ratio-world-china-economy-inflation-figure

Swift, Rocky. "Yen Weakens After Data Shows Japan Posted Record Current Account Deficit," *Bloomberg Businessweek*, March 8, 2012. www.businessweek.com/news/2012–04–03/aussie-dollar-remains-lower-on-concern-rate-gap-to-shrink

Takahashi, Yoshio. "Nissan's CEO Says Yen Still Not Weak Enough," *Wall Street Journal*, February 27, 2012. http://online.wsj.com/article/SB1000142405297020 3833004577248773520182302.html

Twaronite, Lisa, and Deborah Levine. "Australia's Dollar Falls a Fourth Day," *Market Watch*, January 6, 2011. http://articles.marketwatch.com/2011-01-06/markets/30764939_1_flood-waters-rise-currency-australian-dollar

See also:

www.aboutcurrency.com/university/fxcourse/major_currency_pairs_person alities.shtml

www.docstoc.com/docs/52595204/cftc-final-forex-rules

www.forexticket.sg/en/tools/01–01-correlation

www.investopedia.com/articles/forex/10/indicators-fx-traders-must-know.asp

www.netdania.com/Products/live-streaming-currency-exchange-rates/real-time-forex-charts/ChartStation.aspx

http://forexmagnates.com/cftc-finalizes-forex-rules-leverage-reduced-to-150/

http://stockcharts.com/school/doku.php?id=chart_school:technical_indicators

About the Author

MARIO SINGH is a widely sought after forex trader and educator who has been featured many times on CNBC. Using the trading methodologies he now teaches, Mario went from cleaner to successful trader within just three years. Today, Mario has trained over 20,000 people, including institutional traders from ICBC (China's largest commercial bank), on how to profit consistently from forex trading. Besides having written numerous articles for *FX Street*, *Smart Investor*, and *Your Trading Edge*, Mario writes the weekly forex column at one of Singapore's national newspapers, *My Paper*. His weekly articles are posted on his blog, www.mariosingh.com.

He can be contacted at info@mariosingh.com

About the Website

Please visit this book's companion website at www.wiley.com/go/ 17strategies (password: singh123). The website includes these documents to supplement the information in the book:

- Trader quiz (Chapter 5)
- More examples of forex strategies (Chapters 6–10)
- Forex trading journal
- Forex trading flow guide
- Lot size calculators
- Money management risk table
- Goal-setting worksheets
- Goal-setting templates for your first million

 FXPRIMUS 100% BONUS TRADING CREDIT

Get a 100% Forex Trading Bonus and Then Withdraw It
Just fund USD100 or more in your Live FXPRIMUS Forex account to qualify.

Examples:
- Fund USD100 and get USD200 to trade with.
- Fund USD500 and get USD1,000 to trade with.
- Fund USD1,000 and get USD2,000 to trade with.

Fund any amount between USD100 and USD10,000 to receive your corresponding 100% bonus trading credit. The more you fund, the bigger your bonus trading credit.

Visit www.wiley.com/go/17strategies for more details.

Terms and conditions apply.

Index